Ann Storey

Fish   Trees
P. 20   38
         58

Mosaics: Principles and Practice

Joseph L. Young

Mosaics: Principles and Practice

*Frontispiece: Installation of granite and glass mosaic for
Los Angeles County Hall of Records, 1962, by Joseph Young*

 Reinhold Publishing Corporation/New York

With deep appreciation to my family,
friends, and pupils, I dedicate this
book to all those who have the courage
it takes to trust their own creativity.

Type set by Howard O. Bullard, Inc.
Printed by Halliday Lithograph Corporation
Color printed by Princeton Polychrome Press
Bound by Van Rees Book Binding Corporation

CONTENTS

"Get that man's name!"

2

INTRODUCTION

Mosaic alphabet

An Ancient Art Revives

Since the end of World War II, the art of making mosaics has taken firm root in the cultural soil of America. From a handful of dedicated pioneers there has grown a body of hundreds of developing professionals and thousands of lay people who have become interested in doing original and beautiful mosaics as a spare-time activity. Within a few short years every conceivable type of mosaic has appeared in homes, on buildings, and in exhibitions. As with many sweeping movements, most of these first efforts showed all the promise of early enthusiasm but, too often inspired by a rash of doubtful literature, usually lacked in the fundamentals of quality.

Too few of the examples revealed an understanding of the organic design possibilities that can be created with the basic geometric shapes most often available in mosaic. Still fewer recognized that design and execution are an inseparable creative process. With such attitudes prevelant, it became inevitable that a vulgarization of mosaics with "do-it-yourself" kits would follow the same "paint-by-the-numbers" path initiated by the merchandisers of mediocrity. To those who believe in the values of mature artistic expression, there is no greater condemnation of our present cultural achievement than the proliferation of catalogues of prepared drawings designed to take advantage of the beginner's timidity in design by exploiting his fear of being taken as an amateur.

Unfortunately, there are even other groups who have contributed to the confusion regarding the practice of mosaics as an art and craft. The group closest to "painting" attempted to recreate mosaics in the image of their medium by forcing the time-consuming technique of executing mosaics to express the contemporary drive toward "introspective" and spontaneous surface effects at any cost. This necessitated the improvization of pseudo-primitive techniques, which in turn invalidated all content in the work. However, even this basic misunderstanding of the art was overshadowed by the methods of a larger and more obvious group, who drafted on graph paper endless checker-board images as architectural screen walls. This sterile approach quickly became an academic cliché of modern architecture and was little better than those Victorian-inspired murals in which scale designs were farmed out to mosaic workshops for execution. It is this latter group that personified a fallacious post-Renaissance concept in the arts, a concept that fails to cope with the unfortunate practice (born of the Industrial Revolution) of subdividing the arts and crafts into assembly line production.

Despite all these *minor* reactionary forces, there exists a very healthy future for mosaics as an art, which is immensely important to the growth of American art in general. Mosaics, with its orderly use of color, form, and texture is an integrating force in the complex arts of our automated world and could not help but generate some opposition. The rapid passing of this banal exploitation of mosaics only reminds us that a free society, such as ours, must voluntarily develop a broader correlation between artist, educator, and architect. If more inspired expressions in mosaic are to occur in the future, it is to the educator that we must look; for, to the extent that he is able to shake off the remnants of "fine-arts" dicta, he will be able to take up the democratic challenge of advocating all the arts as being essential to man's needs. In the meantime, this expanded edition is written to serve as guide toward that goal, both for the beginner and advanced student.

JOSEPH YOUNG
Los Angeles, 1963

Silver box with wood inlay, Karl Larsson, Santa Fe. Merit award winner, Craftsmen of New Mexico—1960.

4

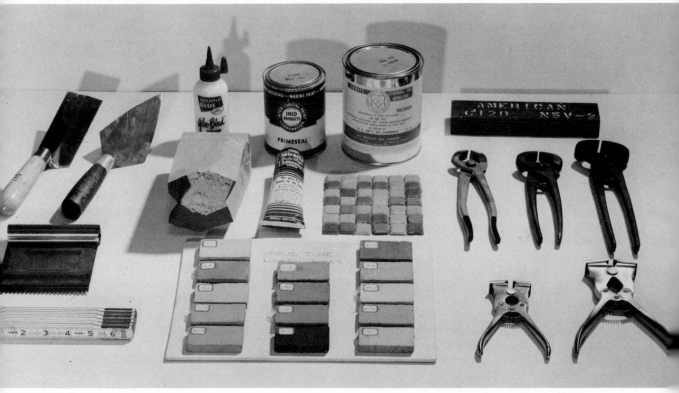

5

For spreading adhesives (left), spatula, trowel, notched spreader; adhesives (top, center) Wilhold glue, sealer, a can and a *tube of ceramic tile adhesive; abrasive stone to file fine cuts of mosaic, and under this, five types of carbiloid-tipped tile cut-* *ters; (center) grouting cement, samples of ¾-inch-square mosaic glass and mineral oxide colors for coloring the grout.*

Tools & Materials

The first requirement is a work area with good light, a sturdy table, and adequate storage space for tools and materials. Select an area that is not accessible to children or pets, and where the flooring can be readily covered with a protective layer of cardboard. A simple shelf arrangement with transparent plastic containers or glass jars is practical for storing colors. An assortment of bowls for mixing grout is necessary, as well as a small garbage can to store magnesite or cement. If you do not wear eyeglasses, inexpensive plastic goggles afford protection when cutting glass, tile, or stone. Tweezers are handy for placing fine cuts, and a screwdriver is useful to remove mistakes after the mastic has dried. Nail polish remover is excellent for removing dried adhesive from the fingers, if you are not allergic.

Pressed Glass or Vitreous Tesserae: This is the least expensive of the Venetian or Mexican glass mosaics. It comes under various brand names (Muranite, Padovan, Pelv, Sarim, Sarma, Saivo, Talia, Vetrital, Vetrum, Mosaico Venetiano, etc.), which are basically similar in that they are machine-produced in 15 to 100 colors and cost between $1.65 to $6.00 per square foot, depending on colors. They come in ¾-inch squares, 225 pieces mounted on 1-foot square sheets of paper, approximately ¼-inch thick with beveled edges to facilitate installation. Before purchasing any quantity of pressed glass mosaics, it is important to know that none of them equal the quality of Byzantine glass (*smalti tipo antico*). Upon comparison, pressed glass appears grainy in molecular structure and the colors pastel in appearance. The grades of quality within the pressed glass brand names can be determined by test cutting several tes-

Many craftsmen use natural rocks, pebbles, and semi-precious stones for making mosaics. In addition to the wide range of natural rock and stones available to residents at the beach, in the desert, or in the country, urbanites can find as many as 16 natural colors of crushed rock or gravel by surveying local building supply dealers. Colored rock or gravel comes in various sizes, ranging from pea-sized gravel called Standard Crush, to 1-inch and 2-inch Crush. Colored rock or gravel is packaged in 100-pound sacks, and one sack will cover approximately 24 square feet about ½-inch thick.

6

Fulget marble pebbles, containers of Byzantine glass mosaic tesserae; (lower left) examples of Lake Como marble mosaic tiles (a prefabricated veneer) and a sample of ¾-inch square mosaic mounted on paper. All of these materials are from Italy.

7

The variety in composition of antique colored glasses suggests that the earliest forms of glass making grew out of metallurgy and/or firing ceramics. Byzantine glass is made up of sand and various combinations of soda, potash, or lead depending upon the particular color and type of glass desired. Since Byzantine glass is an inorganic material, with a minimum coefficient of expansion, it is ideal for all types of architectural uses. (8) Sand and alloys used to make Byzantine glass being melted in furnace in Venice. Temperatures range from 2500° F. upwards. (9)Molten glass being poured onto framed slab from clay crucible. (10) Cutting glass tesserae with a semi-mechanical wheel cutter.

8

serae: the thinner glass mosaic is more difficult to cut accurately. To overcome this tendency to crumble or fracture in unpredictable directions, the cheaper glass has to be scored with a glass cutter before using the tile nippers. *Byzantine Glass Mosaic or Smalti Tipo Antico:* This finest of all glass mosaics is available in a wider variety of sizes, but the most common is ½ x ⅜-inch face and approximately 5/16-inch deep, rectangular in form, with irregular edges. This handmade material comes in a range of 5,000 hues and is preferred by professional mosaicists. The material, manufactured in Europe, is imported in bulk lots retailing on the average of $5.00 per pound (equals $15.00 per square foot) depending upon color, quality, and quantity. *Ceramic Tiles and Marble Tesserae:* There are numerous firms in the United States who manufacture various lines of mosaic tile, glazed and unglazed, suitable for mosaics. These tiles (as well as those imported from Italy, Spain, Puerto Rico, Mexico, etc.) are the

least expensive, approximately $1.00 per square foot and often ideal for the beginner. Marble or Marme tesserae (cubes), manufactured in Italy, are among the most expensive materials used to make mosaics. Casavan-Carrara Marble Co., Inc., 1 Mount Vernon Street, Ridgefield Park, N. J. is one of the principal importers of the material. *Selection of adhesives* is determined by the type of mosaic you are making. Where a utilitarian mosaic is going to be exposed to moisture, as in outdoor swimming pools or patios, it is customary to embed these mosaics in a mortar made from cement mixed with sand and water. For interior mosaics, ceramic tile adhesive, or magnesite, is recommended. When purchasing ceramic tile adhesive, look for the circular hallmark seal on the label, which guarantees the ingredients comply with the U. S. Department of Commerce Standards. Sure-Bond, Miracle 3M (MMM), Armstrong, Chapco, etc., start at $2.00 a quart (enough to cover about 10 square feet). Tile

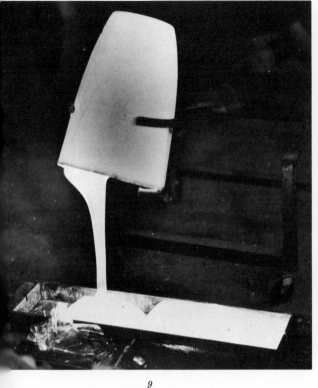

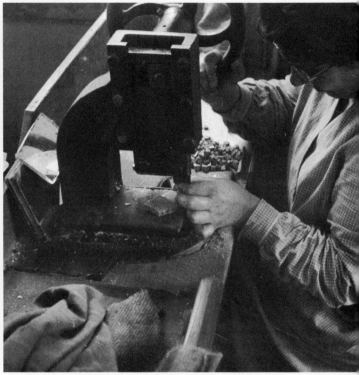

9

10

adhesives are also suitable for smaller mosaics meant to be in contact with water, if you select an adhesive manufactured to resist the alkaline of mortar, and a waterproof grout is employed. Among the names to look for here are Pioneer Latex, Crossfield Products, Armstrong, etc. To further insure the tesserae will not fall out after installation, prime the surfaces of particularly smooth glass with Armstrong J1190. *Supports* for mosaic panels can be made from Novoply or 5-ply Marine plywood. Novoply is an ideal base upon which to make a transportable mosaic panel or table. It can be bought in 4-foot sheets, either 8, 10, or 12 feet long and cut to the required dimensions. Professional mosaicists reinforce this support with a welded iron frame designed to prevent warping, but this need not concern the amateur unless he is tackling a mosaic over six square feet. *Glass or tile cutters*, pincer type with carbiloid-tipped blades come in several well-known brands (approximately $7.00) such as Superior Channe-

lock, Red-Devil, Goldblatt, etc. The Starett Company in Atholl, Massachusetts manufacture an adjustable jaw, double-leverage design that is especially useful for fine cutting; in all instances the carbiloid-tipped blades are recommended, since they will outwear untipped nippers. If the nippers become dull after prolonged use, take them to a tool maker or return to the manufacturer. Carbiloid tips must *not* be ground, but heated and drawn for sharpness.

Sources of Materials and Tools

Tools, adhesives and tesserae can be located by consulting classified directory section of telephone books in larger cities. Suppliers of quality materials are generally listed under "Mosaics," with sub-listings sometimes occurring under "Arts and Crafts," "Tile" or "Ceramic Contractors and Dealers," or "Art Goods, Retail." Below is a list of suppliers who stock most mosaic materials and will fill orders via mail to most locations in the United States.

California: Joseph Young Mosaic Workshop & School, 8426 Melrose Ave., Los Angeles 69; The Dillon Tile Company, 252 Twelfth Street, San Francisco. *District of Columbia:* Standard Art Marble, 117 D Street, NW, Washington. *Florida:* Eastern Tile & Marble Company, Miami. *Massachusetts:* Hatfield's Color Shop, 161 Dartmouth Street, Boston. *Minnesota:* Gager's Handicraft, 1024 Nicollet Avenue, Minneapolis. *New York:* Joseph Mayer Company, Inc., 5-9 West Union Square, New York; Leo Popper and Sons, 143-6 Franklin Street, New York. *Ohio:* Immerman & Son, 1020 Euclid Avenue, Cleveland; Mosaic Tile Company, Zanesville.

Murano Revisited

The manufacture of beautiful glass, once a proud tradition in America, and only lately reviving, has its origins in Europe via Italy. It is almost a cliché to repeat that Italy, particularly Murano, has taught the modern world the art of making glass for mosaics, both through books [1] and the emigration of its artisans. Today, it is still possible for a touring craftsman to visit the Venetian glass factories and see at firsthand the magnificent glassmaking skills practiced almost as they were long before the Renaissance.

One of the best times to visit Venice is during the spring, when the glass factories of the adjacent island of Murano fire up their huge glass kilns after being idle all winter. Motoscafo passage across the lagoon to Murano begins at the Fondamenta Nuove and passes the city cemetery. In addition to visiting a

1. ART OF GLASSMAKING, DIVIDED INTO SEVEN BOOKS, published in Florence, 1612, by A. Nervi. Ten years after the first edition appeared, translations were published in English, Latin and French, and were accepted as authoritative for over a century.

small factory to see a glass worker who is a virtuoso at making a glass clown in less than one minute, it is imperative to see the Glass Museum and the Glass Experimental Station. Traditionally, Italy has always had much in spirit to offer the American craftsman, especially the inspiration of living with a people who appreciate artists as much as the works they create. More specifically, their greatest virtue—a genuine respect for the way a craftsman uses his tools and materials—is deserving of emulation. It is still paramount in the Latin heritage that to create is to live life's purpose.

During my last trip to Italy, at the invitation of the Italian Government, I obtained special permission from the National Association of Glass Manufacturers to make the photographs reproduced below and on page 13. These candid scenes give an intimate glimpse of the glass mosaic factories in Venice and on the famed island of Murano, situated in the lagoon behind Venice proper.

12

11

14

13

16

18

20

Even on a sunny day the ancient island of Murano has a venerable look as the supply barges full of wood for the glass kilns (11, 12 and 13) crowd the entrance to the Fondamenta dei Vetrai (14), where famous names such as Barovier & Toso and Venini (15) grace the lintels of mosaic and glass factories. Inside Sr. Orsoni's glass factory in Venice proper, a master glassmaker removes a gather of glass from the furnace's bye hole with the end of his blowpipe (16) and while it is still white hot, rolls and shapes it on a metal marver (17) prior to mechanically blowing the glass into transparent bladder shapes (18) with a tube of compressed air. When the glass cools, young girls break the vase shapes into smaller flat pieces by hand (19) for later annealing over gold leaf to make the famed ora or gold tesserae so much preferred for ecclesiastical work throughout the world. In another portion of Orsoni's shop, smalti is cut to tesserae size with a semi-mechanical wheel cutter (20), while Venetian ¾-inch-square pressed glass is placed in grid plates (21), and an artisan mounts mosaic on paper by hand (22) for a custom job to be installed in the indirect method. In Italy the craft of making extraordinary mosaic glass is a very lively art.

15

17

19

22

21

WAYS FOR BEGINNERS TO WORK

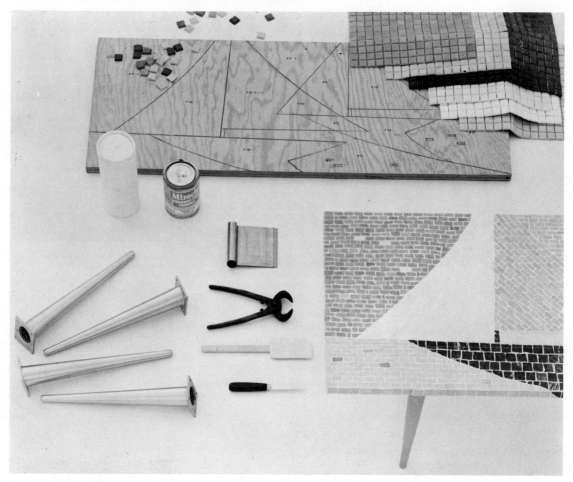

Direct Method

It is wise to gain preliminary experience by making a small trivet in mosaic, or by covering an unglazed ashtray with mosaic. Here, the main principle to master is the application of each tessera directly, one by one, either by pushing them into an area of mastic put on the surface with a spreader, or by buttering each piece separately, and then applying it. In making a mosaic table in the *direct method,* first attach the legs to the panel to provide a working height, then size the top surface of the plywood with a sealer applied with a paint brush. After this dries, pencil in the outline of your design in a simple manner that allows for variety of color and directional placing of the tesserae. While these processes are being carried out, the one-foot square sheets of ¾-inch mosaic should be soaking in a pail of water to facilitate removal of the paper. Next, the paper should be peeled off from the mosaic and the tesserae carefully washed with warm water to remove any excess glue. The mosaic should be thoroughly dried with rags before applying

them, otherwise the ceramic adhesive will not stick effectively. Notice that the tesserae have a face, or front side, which is smooth and a back side, which is beveled along the edges.

If a colored grout is preferred, mineral oxide colors are available at most tile outlets and should be thoroughly dry-mixed with the grout before mixing with water. Final cleaning can be done with steel wool and rags. If the table is for outdoors, or will be washed frequently, use a waterproof grout. Since the project generally takes the beginner approximately 30 to 40 working hours, the lid of the adhesive should be firmly shut when not in use, otherwise the adhesive will dry out. As an added precaution, a protective film of water can be put in the can before closing. Dump out *all* water *before* the mastic is used, as any water remaining will affect the adhesive. To those who want a functionally level table, a carpenter's level is a useful tool. However, the indirect method of installation is recommended if this is the quality you desire to have.

Basic tools and materials required to make a coffee table: approximately seven one-foot-square sheets of ¾-inch-square glass mosaic mounted on paper; a panel of 5-ply Plywood for a base; container of grout; small can of Miracle Ceramic Tile Cement; set of legs; metal spreader to apply adhesive; tile clippers; and two sizes of spatulas, a large one for the grouting process, and a small one for buttering adhesive onto tesserae. Note the way to hold the tessera backside up for buttering (24) and how the spatula is used to apply adhesive. Starting with a corner is the best procedure (25). Work down one side of the table by spreading the mastic out in advance with the larger metal spreader, and place the tesserae with approximately 1/16-inch spacing between (26). Gauging how to cut, an unbuttered tessera is placed over the intersecting line on the design, and the angle to cut marked in pencil. Cutting should be done face side up with the tile cutters biting in rather than across the piece. After completing the table, fill the crevices between the tesserae with cement (a process called grouting). Mix the grout by slowly adding water to the cement until it has the consistency of loose cake batter. The grout is worked quickly into the crevices with the rubber spatula (29) and the excess wiped off with a damp sponge or cloth. Grout has a tendency to dry fast and so work should progress quickly.

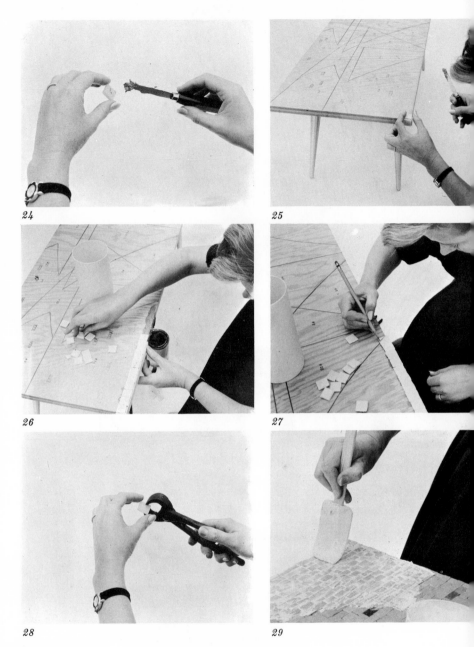

24

25

26

27

28

29

30

31

32

EXAMPLES OF THE DIRECT METHOD

The simplicity of the direct method is best suited for most beginning efforts in the medium. Here are a few examples of first mosaics done by students of the author at his school in Los Angeles.

31—An oriental theme was interpretated in marble and glass mosaic by Anne Frank.

32—The humor of faces conversing with their eyes was designed and executed by Marianne Baumfeld in Venetian glass mosaic.

33—A simple theme of jugs reminiscent of the work of Morandi shows how Jennie Young, the author's mother, used Byzantine glass to achieve an illusion of overlapping transparencies.

34—The antique theme of the dove of peace found so often in the classical works of Ravenna inspired a contemporary interpretation by a student. (See also COLOR PLATE *II, page 19.)*

34

33

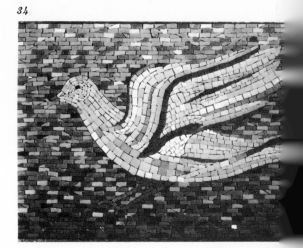

Indirect Method

35

The paperback or *indirect method* of making mosaics is most commonly practiced where a flat and functional surface is desired. Here, a round table was designed and executed by Sylvia Rosenthal for her Palm Springs, California home. The use of a balanced geometric design, based on the face of a compass, eliminated the necessity of executing the mosaic design in reverse. Step-by-step directions are given on the following page.

36

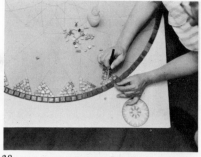

37

38

39

Circular brass frame (1¾ inch wide) was used as guide to cut plywood base, which then screwed into frame (36). Legs were attached. Surface of setting bed inside frame was painted with one coat of sealer (37). Following scale design, the tesserae are pasted with rubber cement to heavy paper, which was patterned and cut along the inside dimensions of the frame (38). Cut with carbiloid-tipped tile cutters (39), each piece was carefully fitted to the next until design was completed (40). Magnesium chloride was mixed with Magnesite powder (41) in a plastic container with a wood spoon to make a lightweight cement (for interior use only). When mixture reached the consistency of wet mortar (42), it was used to fill the setting bed until the Magnesite could be leveled by pulling a board across the surface (43). The completed mosaic was lifted, turned over, placed into position on the magnesite (44), and firmly leveled out by hand (45). After the mosaic had set for five hours, Bestine was applied with a rag to dissolve the rubber cement (46), and paper pulled away (47). Surface was grouted and polished with rags to complete the table.

40

39

42

44

43

45

46

47

COLOR PLATE *II*

THE DIRECT METHOD

A professional example of a mural done in the direct method by Harry Powers of California. Bill Hammon of the Midwest has done church altars in this manner.

49

48

50

The somewhat more complicated procedures involved in making mosaics in the indirect method suggest that this technique be attempted by the advanced student only. On this page are two fine examples of round table mosaics (48 and 50) done in the indirect method by Diederich Kortlang of Puerto Rico, who prefers to set his work in a lightweight cement and polish down the surface by hand. This honing process is generally done with another slab of marble, with various types of sand acting as the abrasive. Note how mosaicist Kortlang uses bold, simple compositions reminiscent of the early Roman work in the Baths of Caracalla, without losing his contemporary touch. At left above (49), the still life by mosaicist Leiss of Italy also employs the soft quality of marble tesserae to compose a handsome still life. For smaller works of this type it is often more practical to lay out the paper-mounted mosaic face down on a smooth surface, surround this with whatever metal or wood frame is planned for, and then pour the grout and cement from the rear, being careful that the piece is reinforced with wire mesh attached to the frame before pouring the cement (see also pages 66 and 67). In the color reproduction on the right (COLOR PLATE III) the author designed and executed the combination Venetian and smalti mosaic for the exterior of his studio entrance. The technique employed here was similar to the method shown on page 18 in that this mosaic was installed over a metal framed and reinforced plywood panel.

Suggestions on Cutting

51

Mosaicist Larry Argiro of New York uses a pair of carbiloid tile clippers to fracture glass mosaic. Maximum leverage is gained with relaxed gripping of tool toward the end of its arm. This is less tiring and establishes a consistent way to measure how much pressure is required for each particular cut.

All cutting is based on variations of the square or circle. In order to plan the cutting of a mosaic, the beginner should experiment within these basic shapes. For example, half a square is two equal rectangles; divide one of these rectangles in half, and two smaller equal squares result. A diagonal line across a square will make two triangles. This also suggests subdivisions that are useful to study. The main value of this approach is that it offers a systematic way to explore the scope and scale of sizes most satisfactory for each particular project.

How well this approach works depends on how the cutting tools are manipulated. Fundamentally, there are two ways to cut mosaic: with a mosaic hammer and chisel or with tile clippers. Both methods are based on a fracturing process. The older system of using a hammer is still preferred by many professionals; however, since custom-made hammers are not available on the American market, the beginner should use a tile cutter.

Familiarity with what the tile clippers can and cannot do comes from practice integrated with study of how the mosaic masterpieces of the past were cut. Techniques of cutting are based on the particular fracturing characteristics of the materials employed. For example, the cutting of many types of marbles, stones, rocks, and pebbles requires power tools that saw, tumble, or grind rather than fracture. Therefore, it is advisable to use these materials either in their natural state or in precut sizes.

Byzantine glass, because of its finer molecular structure, fractures differently from the thinner and less opaque $\frac{3}{4}$-inch squares of mass-produced mosaic. Each color in all grades or qualities of mosaic has a different fracturing characteristic or "cutting feel," and these too should be memorized. Ceramic tile tesserae are easily cut with the spring-type tile clippers, and, generally, are of more even cutting consistency from color to color.

Clean, crisp, and accurate cuts also depend

on how the tessera is held between the cutting blades. The tessera should be held by the thumb and forefinger at a 90° angle to the cutting blades, otherwise the glass will crumble or fracture inaccurately. Normal wastage for beginners learning to cut sometimes runs as high as 50%, but with practice 20% should be maximum. In all instances the scraps should be saved for future work.

When cutting a Byzantine glass tessera into equal parts, exact cuts can be achieved by placing the entire piece between the blades; the ¾-inch glass mosaic squares fracture more accurately if approximately ¼ to ½ of the tessera is inserted between the blades. Do not hold the tile clippers too close to your face while cutting, as flying glass can be dangerous.

It saves time when working on large areas to precut groups of shapes and sizes in advance, and to be sure an adequate range of color is available. Much of the final tactile and optical beauty of a mosaic depends on the self-discipline employed while cutting. In a well-cut mosaic every tessera has its precise place, and the total result gives the impression that all the tesserae are permanently locked into an organic unity. It is when this caliber of cutting skill is combined with a creative use of color perspective that the power of expression in mosaic becomes effective.

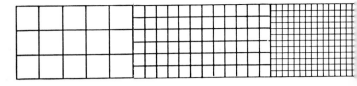

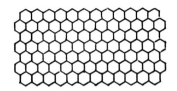

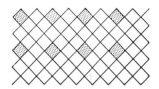

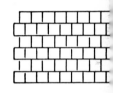

Five examples of ways to cut mosaic: glass mosaic tesserae used primarily in square and rectangular shapes (52); ceramic tile cut in such a way that tri- *angular tesserae appear to dominate the composition (53); stones and pebbles used in their natural state (54); rectangular shaped tesserae assembled in* *a calligraphic or baroque manner (55); and an example where the cutting was subordinated completely to the use of larger grout areas (56).*

52   53   54   55   56

COLOR PLATE *IV*

Bank of the Commonwealth, Detroit, by Saunders Schultz of Clayton, Missouri. Ceramic, mosaic, plastic and stained glass.

When it is recommended that the tesserae of a well made mosaic be locked into an organic unity, this does NOT mean that a "jamming" or "packing-in" of tesserae as tightly as possible is the objective. Quite the contrary, it is the variety of spacing according to the rhythm and form desired that determines a well made mosaic. The spaces between tesserae seldom take up over 10% of the total surface of most mosaics but that 10% is mechanically and aesthetically important beyond its actual ratio. This is called *planning for your grouting in advance,* and a poorly grouted mosaic generally is initiated by poorly planned cutting. The greatest mosaics ever made were created with *minimal* cutting, precisely because the mosaicist achieved the maximum use of materials with minimum effort. Thus, the importance of preparing the design or cartoon with detailed care cannot be overstressed. For with only an outline plan as the sole guide, most beginners arbitrarily fill up the spaces between the lines with variations of textural applications that have little or no relationship to the forms desired.

The Tesseratomic Method of Cutting

Some of the finest examples of beautiful cutting known are the magnificent early Chris-

tian works in Ravenna, Italy, in which the mosaicists consciously made their smalti tesserae rectangular in shape, a size most suitable to working in life-size scale. Today, however, it is the mass-produced, ¾-inch-square Venetian glass that is much less expensive and more readily available. To overcome this serious limitation of shape, the author originated the Tesseratomic Method to provide his students with a means to eliminate the static and non-directional character of the square-shaped Venetian glass by planning the cutting in ways that activate the directional possibilities of the tesserae.

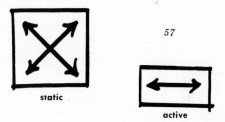

57

The difference between the grid system of cutting illustrated on page 23 and the diagrams below is that the grid method cannot do more than offer stilted checker-board images while the Tesseratomic Method offers the creative freedom of an organic application of geometric principles.

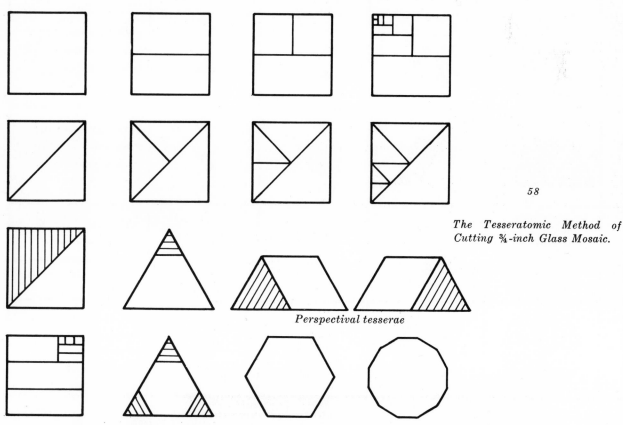

58

The Tesseratomic Method of Cutting ¾-inch Glass Mosaic.

Perspectival tesserae

Note the logical progression from square shape to circle.

The chart below illustrates how the Tesseratomic Method of cutting is organized into a modular system of equally diminishing sizes; *i.e.*, a vocabulary of cutting that allows the mosaicist to plan such practical considerations as the scale of tesselation according to the viewing depth of his work. Although the mosaicist very often assembles his work from a viewing depth of approximately two feet, the prefabrication must be done in a manner that anticipates the true viewing depth of the completed mosaic in place. When working in the indirect method, the mosaicist has the added task of getting accustomed to working the image in reverse. Also briefly noted on the chart below are the major historical periods that contributed toward the evolution of these basic shapes and some of the attendant characteristics.

VOCABULARY OF CUTTING ¾-INCH GLASS				
	100 feet	50 feet	25 feet	15-0 feet	Recommended viewing distance for various sizes of tesserae
1					CLASSIC Greek and Roman square: order stability
2					BYZANTINE Early Christian rectangle: direction movement
3					CONTEMPORARY Industrial Revolution triangle: force aggression
4					RENAISSANCE-BAROQUE Perspectival trapezoid: depth volume
5					VICTORIAN hexagon: compromise between Classic and Age of Reform
6					AGE OF ENLIGHTENMENT Reformation circle: radiation persuasion

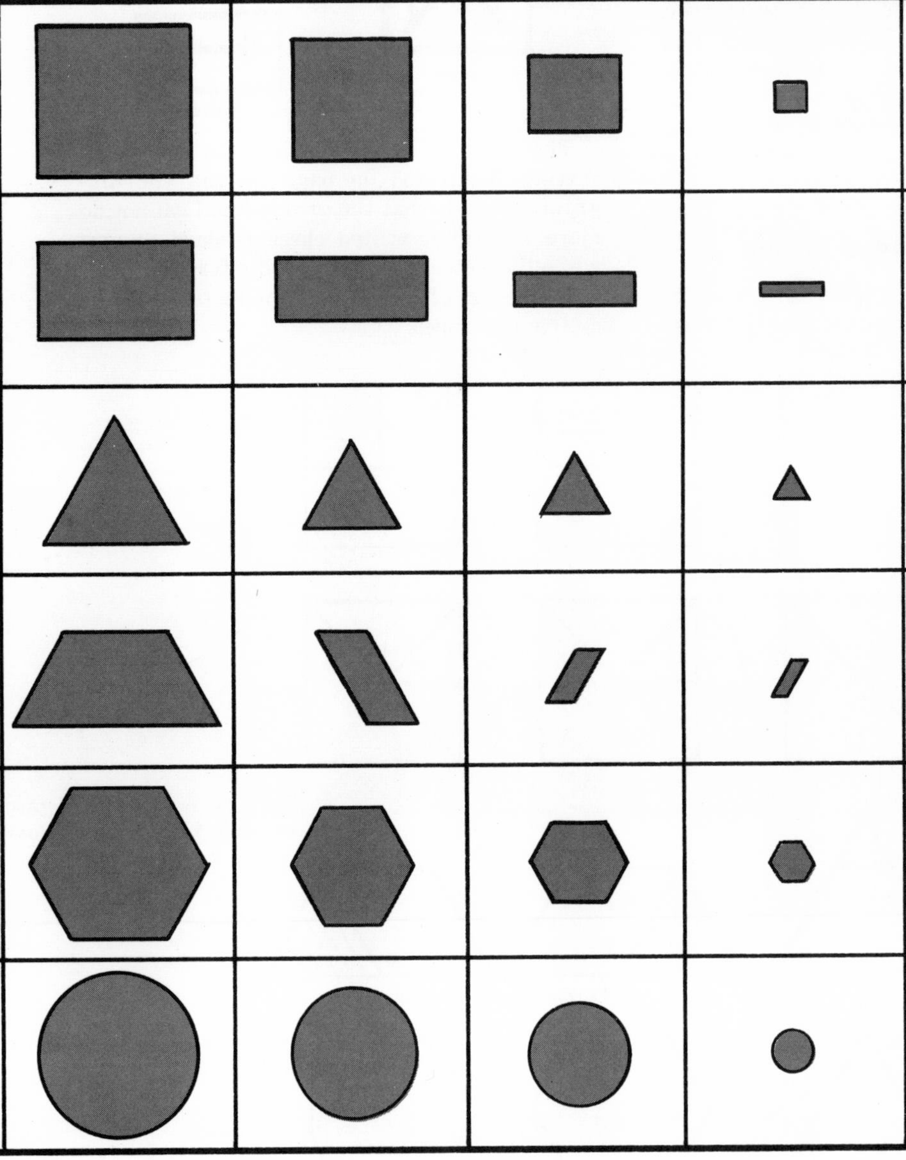

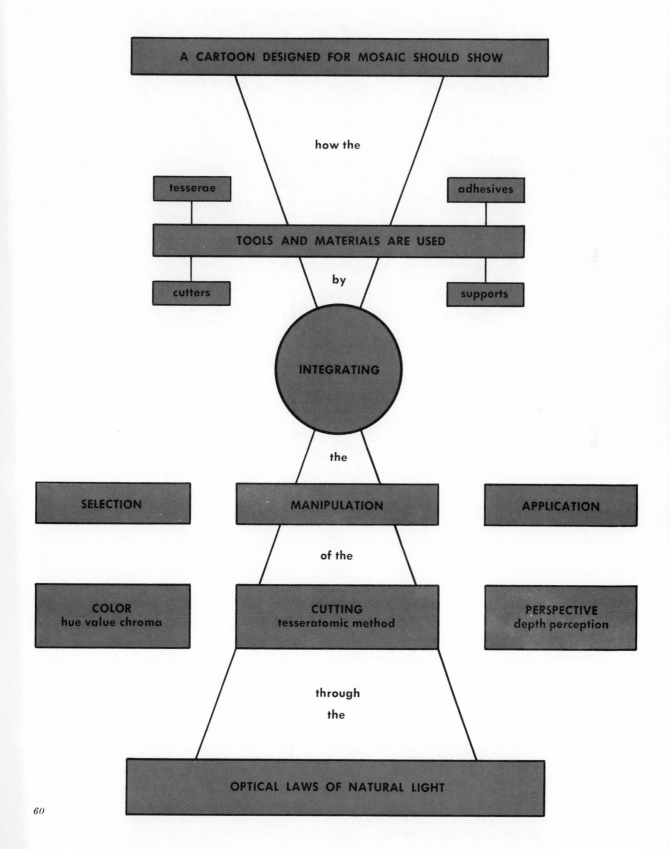

61

No theoretical system of cutting is of any value unless it functions to aid in designing. Since the Tesseratomic Method differs drastically from planning work for spontaneous media such as watercolor, oil or gouache, it is essential that the design for a mosaic be of a quality that justifies the effort required in execution. Concern with the use of durable materials to achieve permanent results automatically takes more time. Such a design should plan for the cutting (as illustrated above with a student drawing) in a coordinated sense; *i.e.*, by developing the volume of each form as opposed to drawing outlines. This is especially important, since the latter tech-

nique for the beginner tends to encourage the use of arbitrary (and often meaningless) cutting to fill up areas without regard to color modulation or the relationship of textures to the directional nature of forms depicted in mosaic. Again, as above, only by first massing in the forms in color was the student able to prepare a planned use of perspectival tesserae. The drawing was done by laying a sheet of tracing paper over a fixed pastel drawing done previously in color. This technique allows the beginner to dissociate the cutting from the color long enough to appreciate how they must be integrated during the execution, to create the optical illusion of three-dimensions.

The process of how a mosaic is made can be stated in three words: *selection, manipulation* and *application*. The various colors that are selected have to be manipulated (formed and shaped by cutting) and then adhered to a support in a perspectival manner (see chart, page 25). The illustrations below show how the illusion of depth in a mosaic is obtained by cutting the tesserae to conform to the lines going to a diminishing point. It also helps to remember that depth in a mosaic can most easily be created by following the generalization of cutting the tesserae smaller for those forms higher in the picture plane. In this way distance is achieved by the use of a series of relative sizes. The series of equally diminishing shapes shown in the diagram on page 26 indicates this use as well as for gauging the normal viewing distances comfortable to see various sizes of tesserae. Since the uses of perspective in making mosaics can be nearly infinite, the beginner is recommended to acquaint himself with this fascinating subject by referring to *How To Use Creative Perspective* by Ernest W. Watson and *Pencil Techniques in Modern Design* by Atkin, Corbelletti and Fiore (Reinhold). For now, the fact worth stressing is that the mosaic cartoon must contain all the above advance information if it is to be of any value.

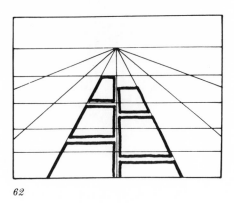

62

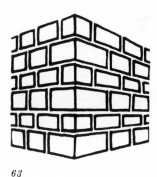

63

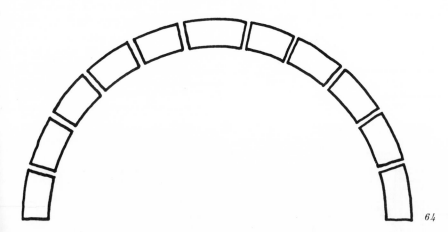

64

Whenever possible the neophyte in making mosaics should work directly in color, always working toward reassociating in his mind that *color* is *value* and the manipulation of *color-value* is how *form* is created. For purposes of simplification the fundamental nature of color in mosaic could be stated: *color is value is form!* In earlier times it was not necessary to emphasize this fact, since art and its reproduction had not yet suffered the divisive over-specialization that commenced with the Renaissance. With the invention of the camera and the photo-engraving process, man began to accept visual half-truths offered in black and white reproductions; *i.e.*, color was dissociated from form by reproducing the original color image in values from black to white. In mosaics of quality, color functions best when it creates form. Once this essential is fully understood, then composing forms in design (or preparing a cartoon) is no longer a major problem. This too is what is meant when artists admire the integrated way children have of seeing form and color as one. Once it is possible to design one form in mosaic then the next step of composing many forms into a design makes it possible for the beginner to project his personal imagery through an effective use of the medium.

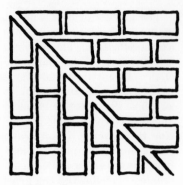

67. Mitered corner

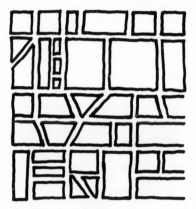

68. Mixed pattern

65. Labyrinth

69. On-edge cuts

66. Herring bone

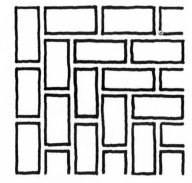

70. Expanding rectangles

Suggestions on Color

Although the potential combinations of colors in mosaics are nearly infinite, the beginner should not be discouraged because the basic approach to understanding the use of color does not have to be complicated. First, let us see how the major scientific color systems generally agree on what mosaicists have known for generations, *i.e.*, that color, especially in mosaics, has a strong psychological effect upon most people. Except to those who are color-blind, color appears either warm or cool and thus can be made to seem to advance or recede in an image, depending upon how the color is used.

Since the juxtaposition of warm and cool colors is what creates the illusion of depth, then color, particularly in mosaic, is inseparable from linear perspective. The directional nature and size of tesserae take care of this; things that are small seem to recede and things that are large seem to advance. Since the art of making mosaics is an art of using color, there is a basic rule that applies: *Hue is Chroma is Value is Form,* or, reading the rule in reverse, *Form is Value is Chroma is Hue.* Although this multiple construction sounds like a parody of Gertrude Stein, the rule as stated means exactly what it says, *i.e.*, forms in mosaic are most successfully realized when the mosaicist understands that these elements are inseparable. More specifically, the functions of hue (color), chroma (intensity), and value (lightness or darkness) must be well coordinated in a mosaic if forms are to be convincingly created.

The beginner who clings to the habit of filling in mosaics between traced outlines blocks his own development of color knowledge, since this approach ignores how colors function in reality as hues in various combinations of value and chroma. Most libraries have detailed information on the principal systems of color and how they work, but time can be saved if study is devoted to works of artists such as Gustav Klimt, Vincent van Gogh, Paul Cézanne, and Georges Seurat. These artists employed systems of juxtaposing colors; a careful analysis of their compositions reveals how they created forms in color without the use of outlines.

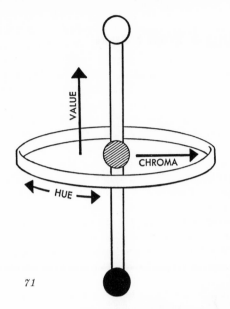

71

The three commonly recognized dimensions of color. Hues run in a circle about a neutral gray axis. Values run in vertical scales from light to dark. Chromas (intensity or saturation) run in horizontal scales from pure color to gray.

Linear delineation employing the size and directional placement of tesserae is coordinated with Form is Value is Chroma is Hue, i.e., light creates shadow on the cylinder, which is described in mosaic by starting on the left (a) with a narrow vertical row of dark blue stones and working to the center high light of the cylinder (b) with all the chroma steps between the small dark blue stones and large light pink stones.

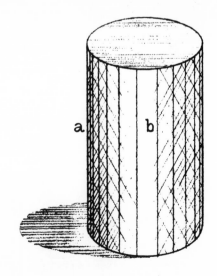

72

Doing a Wall Panel

Many beginners starting a wall panel try to emulate painting, an approach that unfortunately resembles neither painting nor mosaic. One practical way to avoid this pitfall is to study the making of mosaics as an art, an art that developed its own particular craft because it can do what other art forms cannot. Mosaic is an architectural art form in which a bold and creative use of the tools and materials is essential. Here, George Millar, well-known California mosaicist, demonstrates how he designs and executes a wall panel in the direct method. The design, in this case, stressed an interpenetra-

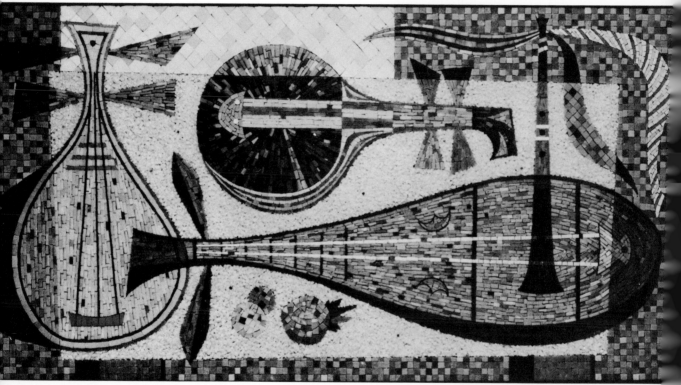

73

tion of shapes in which the color, values, and planes are integrated. The final accents of the musical instruments were achieved by highlighting the strings with specially selected brass strips. Such a panel is not beyond the abilities of many beginners if emphasis is placed on a creative approach. Mosaic is an art medium that takes time to execute. To retain a spontaneous expression is always a problem. The technique of execution requires a coordination of manual skill, patience, and knowledge, three disciplines that should always be excited by the challenge of creative ideas.

(74) Working from a scaled sketch, the mosaicist outlines the forms in charcoal so that he can rework the shape relationships while planning how he will lay the mosaic.

74

(75) Great care, patience and skill are devoted to cutting; to use the tool efficiently, the tile clippers are held with the head of the nippers facing the hand holding the tesserae. The tile clippers can be operated equally well left handed or right handed.

75

76

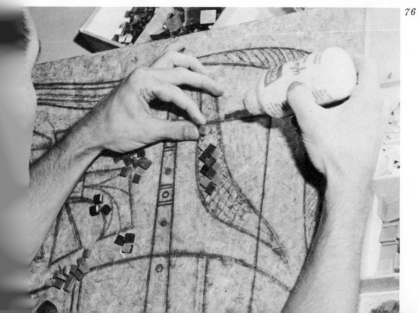

(76) Wilhold Glue is applied in a small dab to the specific place on the design where the tessera is to be placed. The tesserae are placed face upward and exactly where they are wanted. Since the glue is quite strong when it dries, corrections are difficult to make afterwards.

Grouting a Wall Panel

Ever since the introduction of mosaics to a wider audience, many who are experimenting in the medium have been confused by the myriad claims about the functions and purposes of grout. This fine finishing cement, traditionally used by professionals since the 1850's as an adhesive filler between the remaining crevices or joints of the tesserae when a mosaic is completed in the *indirect* method, has generally been badly misused by beginners doing a wall panel in the *direct* method for the first time.

Grouting definitely has a subordinate role when mosaics are done in the *direct* method as practiced today. Since it does not act as the adhesive, it serves no particular function other than to give the beginner a false sense of "professional" fulfillment. In fact, the sharp, crisp appearance of a wall panel done on wood for interior use is often completely lost with the application of grout. Despite much literature to the contrary, the importance of grouting of an interior wall-panel has been grossly exaggerated.

Naturally, grouting is absolutely essential if functional surfaces are being completed in either the direct or indirect method. Although not until the 1930's did a specially prepared grout come into wide use, today a commercially manufactured grout is made by milling titanium dioxide, an intensely white pigment, with white Portland cement. Precisely because the stark, antiseptic white of these commercially prepared grouts does not stain or darken easily, they tend to make mosaics appear more suitable for sanitary rather than aesthetic purposes.

When each tessera is surrounded with a dead white cement, the grouting tends to optically "bleed out" the color intensity of the image. In no case will such grouting serve to cover up all the sins of sloppy cutting. To the contrary, grouting a haphazardly executed mosaic in white will only tend to emphasize the cutting mistakes. These warnings are not meant to imply that grouting should never be used in doing a first wall panel mosaic. When used, however, there should be sound functional or aesthetic purposes in mind. Grout can help complete a mosaic only if either or both of these purposes are planned for.

One of the more important recent contributions to the field has been the development of a beautiful range of metallic oxides or permanent coloring pigments that allow an experienced mosaicist to emphasize or minimize warm and/or cool color effects by the addition of these basic colors into the grout. It is also possible to mask off each area of a mosaic separately and employ a number of different colored grouts and/or stains.

Today it seems self-evident that colored grouts provide greater flexibility of design for the mosaicist. The joints between tesserae may be accented by using sharply contrasting colors within the same or separate fields of color. Conversely, the joints can be de-emphasized or made to "die" into the wall by using a colored grout keyed to match the mosaic colors in the field. This latter effect is especially useful when the mosaicist wishes to minimize the static or nondirectional character of a geometric grid pattern. Another advantage in using colored grouts is the resulting low maintenance costs when the work is completed.

Because it can be a messy job, grouting should be done in those areas of a home or workshop where tracking up the premises does not create a major cleaning problem. Plenty of newspaper laid under the mosaic helps, but thin plastic sheeting is still better, as it is waterproof.

A white, stain-resistant epoxy grout was introduced in 1962. It is a two-component sys-

The six photographs on the right show a technique of great interest to many beginners. In this case Lolita Guiral, a former student of the author, having already done a number of successful traditional mosaics, elected to outline the shapes with brass stripping. In this type of project brass is generally the "polished" or "brushed" variety about ⅛ inch thick by ¼ inch high, available at the larger hardware stores. These dimensions are best suited for easy forming of contours with pliers (77), cutting with strong wire shears, and shaped to correspond with the planned outline as well as the approximate height of the tesserae to be placed against the brass. After the shaping and cutting was completed, the brass was pinned into position with small brass brads hammered in to hold the brass upright. Once the brass outlines were positioned, the forms within these outlines were just as carefully developed as if there were no outlines used as a guide, and the forms were created out of color juxtaposition. The brass outline served only as an accent. Photo 78 shows grout being poured over the panel, and 79 shows the grout being spread with a spatula. After setting, excess grout was sponged off (80). In photo 81 a clean shoe brush was used the following day to polish the surface. Photo 82 shows the final result; in this case mosaicist Guiral shows her interest in the combination of ceramic with smalti.

77

78

79

80

81

tem in which the base and activator are mixed for 15 minutes and then applied in much the same manner as conventional grout. Pot life at 70 degrees is about 90 minutes. It generally takes three practice jobs before a craftsman can develop the proper skill for its application. The new material goes under the brand name of Bond and is manufactured by the Garland-White Company of San Leandro, California.

Care should be taken to lay all the necessary tools and equipment in advance. Many a fine mosaic has been ruined in the last half hour of effort for want of water or a sponge to control the drying of the grout. Mixing bowls, plastic sponges, a plastic dish-scraper and a large container of clean cool water are essential and should be at hand before grouting begins.

The coloring agent of metallic oxides should be thoroughly mixed into the white grouting cement *dry, and before* a 70 to 30 proportion of water and Wilhold glue is added to make the mixture of pancake-batter consistency. The addition of Wilhold or Elmer's glue helps prevent the grout from drying out too rapidly and cracking. As the photographs show, the grout should be swiftly distributed over the entire surface evenly by briskly rubbing into all the crevices between the tesserae with a plastic dish scraper. After it has been allowed to set for from 10 to 20 minutes, depending upon the humidity of the weather, the excess should be thoroughly sponged off until the surface is clean and all pinholes filled.

The freshly grouted mosaic should be permitted to sit overnight, preferably a full 24 hours, to thoroughly dry out. The thin haze left on the surface can be removed by polishing the surface with dry rags, paper or a clean shoe brush. Many mosaicists prefer to complete the job with brick and tile cleaner and then seal the grout with Stone Glamour or a silicone preparation.

82

These photographs illustrate the type of advanced project which interests beginners who have completed a wall panel and understand the fundamentals of designing a mosaic for execution. Here, mosaicist Ray Rice of Sausalito, California is shown creating a *utilitarian* mosaic table and an *integrated* mosaic over a fireplace for the Braun and Heller residences in San Francisco. In both cases, the indirect method of first pasting the tesserae down on paper was employed. Note how the artist subdivided the paper-mounted mosaic into sections to facilitate installation. On smaller projects of this nature, it is possible for the artist to do the installation; however, on larger mosaic murals it is advisable to employ the professional skills of union tile setters familiar with installing mosaics. Also note that the artist started the installation at the base of the fireplace and worked upward. This is standard procedure in America; in Europe mosaics are installed by starting at the top and working down. Each system has its advantages. The American technique prevents the mosaic units from sliding down the wall, an event that sometimes occurs when installing a mosaic mural during a very wet day. The European system saves time on larger projects as it requires only one wash-up of the installed mosaic after the paper is removed, a most important advantage when the mosaic is so large that it requires more than one day to install.

85

84

Projects for Home and Family

87

(87) *For those who prefer a rugged outdoor feeling in their living room, this iron and mosaic fireplace, designed and executed by David Tolerton and Louisa Jenkins of Big Sur, California, is a fine example of effective collaboration between sculptor and mosaicist.*

(88) *Rock and glass mosaic mural designed and executed for the dining room of Joseph Mitchell's home in Los Angeles by Kayla Selzer.*

(89) *Mosaic and plaster bas-relief mural designed and executed by Hugh Wiley for the foyer of the Perrin home in New York City.*

88

89

90

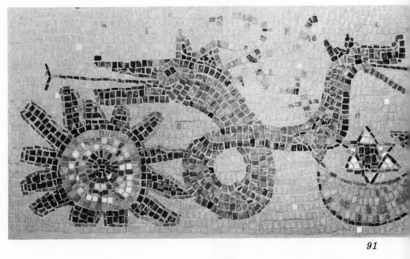

91

92

93

94

(90) Here is an interesting example of what can be done with a door-knob; designed and executed by Kayla Selzer of Los Angeles.

(91) Fritz Faiss, noted artist of Northridge, California, demonstrates his well-known versatility in this "Seamonster" mosaic fantasy for the swimming pool of the Helwig home; this was executed in a variety of Byzantine mosaic colors, including gold leaf tesserae.

(92) An example of mosaic tile flooring manufactured by the Capoferri brothers of Bergamo, Italy. This material, reminiscent of ancient Greek floors, has found wide use as patio flooring both in America and Europe, and goes under the name of Fulget. Here the stones are embedded in a cement form and the tiles produced can be arranged into many designs.

(93) Garden planters can take on a handsome durability when covered with mosaic, as exemplified by this imaginative installation done in ¾-inch square mosaic for the Bantam Cock Restaurant entrance in Los Angeles.

(94) Byzantine mosaic has found application also in contemporary lamp bases as designed by Nicholas and Larry Argiro of New York. Here smalti, ¾-inch glass mosaic, and brass were combined.

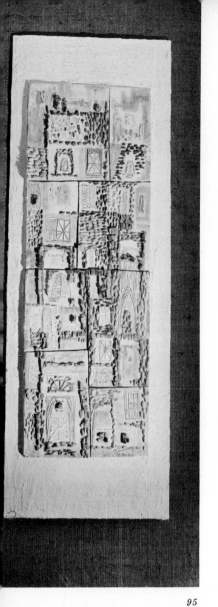

95

96

(95) An original combination of materials was worked out in this "City Scene" by ceramist Lois Stearns, by superimposing Italian-made smalti on hand-made clay tesserae.

(96) Mosaics done in marble have a subtle appeal that is sometimes deceptive. Although they often are done in a simple, direct manner, the design and execution requires the full abilities of a top professional. This "Unicorn," done by Joseph Lasker, demonstrates that a fine mosaic requires more than craft to become a work of art.

(98) Sculptural effect obtained in the smalti mosaic mural by Joseph Young for the Jeff Cameo residence in Beverly Hills, California, 1960.

(97) In both the "Lobster" and "The Birds," Lois Stearns moulded clay into units that were glazed and fired; a technique that can be traced as far back as the Sumerians, nearly 5,000 years ago.

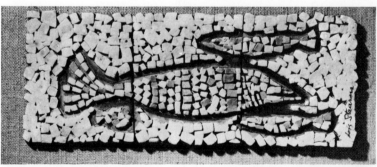

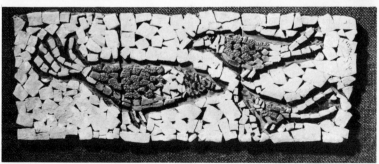

97

99

99. One of the early pioneers in the revival of mosaics, Jeanne Reynal of New York utilizes her exceptional talents to create an exciting entrance that welcomes visitors to the residence of Mr. and Mrs. McKnight in Scarsdale, New York, 1958.

100

100. Baltazar Korab is one of the nation's top architectural photographers. Despite a busy schedule he found time to employ his architectural training to collaborate with his wife on the designing and execution of this brass and ceramic mosaic for the fireplace of their new home in Birmingham, Michigan.

102. Sam Weiner Jr., who teaches art at Columbia University and has done major mural commissions throughout the country, turned his gifted hand to building the shower walls in his own New York home with 4 x 4 glazed tile in blues, greens, white and black. Weiner deliberately broke the tiles to overcome the grid pattern and then installed the tesserae directly.

103. Kayla Selzer of Los Angeles, California is a ceramist who has worked with mosaic frequently. In this commission for the Browne residence in Bel Air, California, she built up the forms in magnesite over chicken wire to develop a bas-relief over the splashboard—a colorful addition to the kitchen.

104. In the outdoor patio area of their home in Birmingham, Michigan, Mrs. Baltazar Korab designed and executed this elegant birdbath fountain: a treat for the birds in fine weather and color note for the eye in the grayer winter months.

102

103

101

104

101. The ancient technique of using flowing water over the surface of mosaic was applied in the entrance foyer of this contemporary home owned by Mr. and Mrs. Kent Oppenheimer of Los Angeles. William Bray, AIA, was the architect and Joseph Young designed and installed the mosaic.

105

106

The sharing of esthetic experiences does not have to be vicarious, especially with the possibilities offered through the medium of mosaic. Making a mosaic as a family, or group, project can offer great satisfaction to participants of all ages. On the left above, artist Emmy Lou Packard is shown assisting two of the 560 children from kindergarten to the sixth grade who participated in making a 126 square foot mosaic mural for the Hillcrest Elementary School in San Francisco. They worked in shifts of six children and completed the work in 27 days. Beach pebbles, broken ceramic, stained glass, abalone shell, and glass mosaic were applied in the direct method with 3-M ceramic tile adhesive (CTA-11) onto seven panels of ¾-inch exterior grade plywood (which were later bolted to the wall).

107

Projects for Schools

Each year nearly 300 schools throughout the nation originate cooperative mosaic mural projects. Among the many excellent ones are two recent examples of particular interest. The first is an ambitious work by the Art III class of the Maine West High School in Des Plaines, Illinois, under the supervision of Richard Meyers (107); the second was supervised by Marie Hempy of the Starr King School for Exceptional Children in Sacramento, California (108).

The Maine West mural is of particular importance because it exemplifies the immense inpact mosaics have had on education, as well as the community at large. In this new high school without any architectural art the students demonstrated that creativity can once again become a traditional civic function. Fifteen plywood panels 18 inches by 4 feet were combined into a 22½-foot long surface

that followed the curve of the auditorium entrance wall. Korsin Crafts of Niles, Ohio supplied the materials as well as technical guidance.

The Starr King School mural, although equal in physical scope, was a project of quite a different nature in that the children who worked together are handicapped and were able to work only for short periods of time. Because of their various afflictions (blindness, deafness, mental retardation, cérebral palsey, etc.), it took a unique collaborative effort to succeed. The instructor, Marie Hempy, describes being inspired by the children's letting her help them make their new school beautiful. Tactile as well as visual qualities were stressed so that the blind as well as the sighted could appreciate this work in honor of Mr. Laurel Ruff, the man who made this very special school possible.

108

109

(109) A full-scale mosaic cartoon done in pastel on double-ply, non-shrinking, toned paper. Tesserae were mounted directly on paper after cartoon was cut up for prefabrication. Note the one-inch equals one-foot scale study on the right; and how the full-scale cartoon on the left was drawn in reverse for the final installation; the cartoon is always done backwards in the indirect method, so that when the completed prefabricated sections are turned over into the cement during installation, the final mural is identical to the first sketch. This mosaic mural of Byzantine glass was designed and executed for Don Bosco Technical High School, South San Gabriel, California, by Joseph L. Young, 1956. Barker and Ott, AIA, Architects. Installation by Premier Tile & Marble Company.

Doing a Cartoon for a Mural

Making a full-scale cartoon, to be executed in either the direct or indirect method, is a procedure essential for the beginner to master. It is here that the coordination between juxtaposition of colors and cutting the tesserae is planned. Only the most experienced professional mosaicists have enough knowledge to successfully create a mosaic without first doing a cartoon. In the past, cartoons for mosaic murals were first done on paper in gouache, or watercolor, and an outline tracing of the design made to transfer either onto a special paper for mounting the tesserae, or onto the wall prepared for installation. This was preceded by a thorough scale study in color in which the mosaicist strictly adhered to using only those colors available in the mosaics at hand. However, since most contemporary artists generally do not embed their work into cement with a grout, unless making a utilitarian surface, it becomes a great time saver when making a wall panel to draw directly on the supporting board with square sticks of pastel colors and/or with a square-nibbed mechanical marking pen. The same is true of large mosaics to be done in the indirect method. Better results can be obtained by most beginners if the outline concept is avoided, as the filling in between outlines tends to produce a mechanical-looking image. Here, time can be saved by doing the cartoon in color directly on the paper to which the tesserae will be mounted; middle-toned papers are best suited to this purpose. A plastic spray fixative will prevent the pastels from smudging. It is best to work boldly on the general concept and then develop details. But most important, think in terms of mosaic as you draw; instead of using the sweeping continuous movements more common to drawing and painting, the pastels or marking pen should be manipulated with the fingers so that the same sweep is expressed in a series of short, staccato-like strokes that swell

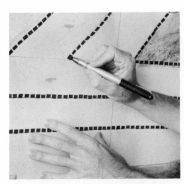

110

111

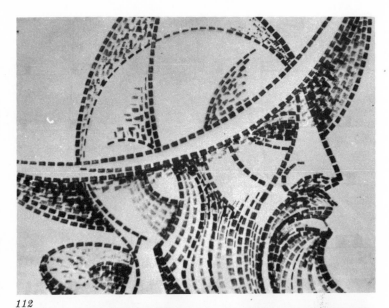

112

Other methods of preparing a cartoon suitable for translation into a mosaic mural are illustrated in photos 110, 111 and 112, in which the author demonstrates the use of the Flomaster ink pen to delineate a preliminary black and white study. In 113 the well-known New York muralist, Lumen Martin Winter, scales a ladder in his studio to detail in full scale each tessera for his monumental 17 x 51-foot mural for the main lobby of the AFL-CIO Building in Washington, D. C. (see also page 80). Note that here too the mural cartoon is done in reverse of the completed work.

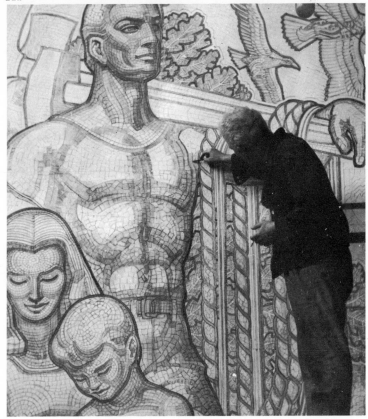

113

and diminish in size, thereby indicating each tessera quickly and clearly as to shape, color, and its relationship to its neighboring tessera. The square-shaped pastels are ideal for this purpose since they are relatively inexpensive and match the approximate width of the most commonly used Byzantine glass tesserae. Also, the pastel color scale as shown in 109 is more

than adequate to indicate most over-all color combinations, if it is assumed an elaboration of color will take place during the final selection and cutting of tesserae for mounting. On this page is a series of suggested drawing exercises which can be used as a guide for those beginners interested in developing their own way to do a cartoon.

Executing and Installing a Mural

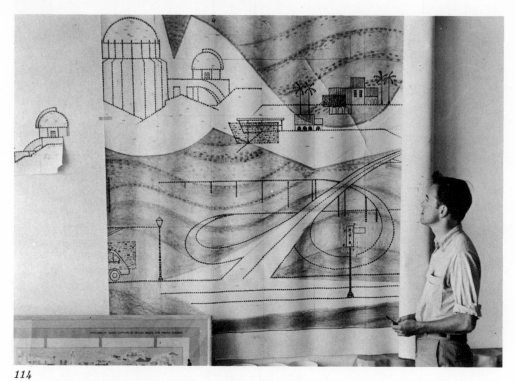

114

The author commenced design of this 6 x 36-foot cantilevered mosaic mural by number-
ing sections and planning how to cut them up as the drawing of the cartoon progressed.

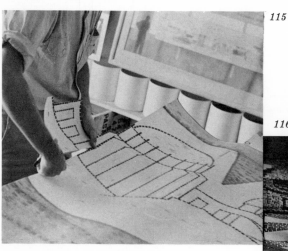

115

116

(115) After expanding the
1-inch equals 1-foot scale color
study into a full-scale cartoon
on heavy double-ply paper, the
entire cartoon was cut into pre-
determined units one foot square
each for the mounting of the tes-
serae on the paper. Non-shrink-
ing paper was used to assure
accuracy of the final dimensions.

(116) Stone by stone the Byzan-
tine tesserae were laid out in a
preliminary mock-up directly on
the sectionalized cartoon to co-
ordinate color, seaming, cutting,
and scale.

117

118

119

120

121

The tesserae were fractured with a mosaic hammer and chisel (117) and then mounted on the paper (118-120), illustrating the indirect method of execution. The completed detail (121) is ready for checking against the cartoon before stacking and storage.

122

123

(122) The mural was reassembled on the floor at the site of installation for a final check. Here the author is shown making final adjustments of the seams.

(123) After the author and head tile setter, Ira Cooper, reviewed the blueprint procedure for installation, the units of the prefabricated mosaic were picked up from the floor and placed on a tile-setter's work bench, where each unit was buttered with ¼-inch layer of colored grouting cement.

124

125

126

A similar coat of cement (124) was evenly troweled onto the cantilevered panel in preparation for the prefabricated one-foot square units (125). Each piece was tamped into the cement with a hammer and block (126), and checked to see if it was level with its neighbor. Notice that the installation occurred from bottom to top.

127

128

Once all the units were in position, the cement was allowed to set for forty-five minutes before the paper was moistened with water and removed (127). The surface was then cleaned by scrubbing with water to remove remnants of glue and excess grout. Several days later the mural was given a final muriatic acid scrub-down (128)—six parts water to one part acid, use with extreme caution—and polished with dry rags.

129

Mosaic mural for main lobby of Los Angeles Police Facilities Building, designed and executed by Joseph L. Young; Welton Becket, FAIA, & Associates, Architects; installed by Premier Tile & Marble Company and AFL Tile Setters Local No. 18 of Los Angeles.

130

131

132

Monumental Mural for Midland

One of the largest and most unusual religious mosaic murals in the nation was installed in 1961 by Joseph Young for the newly completed Presentation of the Blessed Virgin Mary Church in Midland, Pennsylvania. The 1,500-square-foot work, which included the backgrounds for two low altars, was initiated by architect Joseph F. Bontempo, AIA, of Rochester, Pennsylvania. The depiction of the Presentation of Our Lady in the Temple as a child is an unusual Biblical theme that has challenged such great ecclesiastical masters as Titian.

All the prefabricated sections were assembled in the artist's California studio and specially transported across the country for installation by the Rampa Tile & Marble Company of Pittsburgh. Research, design and execution by the artist took over a year. Nearly one million separate pieces of glass were set by hand. Basing his composition on architect Bontempo's structural plan, Joseph Young oriented his grouping of figures on an optical armature that incorporates the main altar as a fulcrum, thereby interpreting the relation of the two major faiths of the Bible in a contemporary manner. This monumental work, which occupies the full 34 x 32-foot reredos wall behind the main altar, is the first major interpretation of this subject in the United States.

Above condensed from article by William M. Rimmel in the *Pittsburgh Post-Gazette*, July 22, 1961.

133

Installation of major murals requires detailed planning of each step. Not only must creative execution on a teamwork basis follow the preparation of an imaginative design (130), but the very layout of the mural in advance of installation (131) allows for color modulations. In this case local artists Beatrice Marciniak and Ben Kaye were invited to participate by assisting the eight-week installation process under the guidance of the artist. Great precision was required to properly align and place each section on the wall according to the master plan; in illustrations 132 and 133 the tilesetters are shown skillfully cleaning the paper mounting from the surface. To increase the optical warmth of the figures done in Byzantine smalti, a deep brown metallic oxide grout was employed while the background blue field of specially cut Venetian glass was accentuated with the use of a deep blue grout color. Over 300 colors were employed and further sparkle was created by a generous use of gold accents throughout and by a final staining of the grout in details. After a light buffing with a very fine steel wool, a light coat of silicones and wax was applied to preserve the color of the grout while reducing future maintenance to a minimum. Murals of this scale generally need an annual dusting and a bi-annual washing with clear water and sponges. Detergents and soaps are to be avoided in most interior murals of this scale as they require too much water to rinse away. Illustration 134 shows the total mural in progress, and 135 the mural as it appeared on dedication day, a major cultural event for this community of 10,000.

135

The Mosaic Technique in Other Media

136

After the main forms of the bas-relief were carved (136), a ¾-inch deep setting bed for the mosaic was routed out of the wood, and the Byzantine tesserae cemented into position with Ceramic Tile adhesive (137). Next, the untinted grouting cement was mixed in a plastic container and swiftly brushed into the crevices between the stones (138), and the excess wiped off with a sponge. The final step of staining the wood to bring out the grain (139) also acts as a preservative for the wood while darkening the color of the grout. Completed panel is opposite.

137

138

Wood — Mosaic — Sculpture
by Charles Schlein

As a wood sculptor, I became intrigued with the idea of incorporating wood and mosaic. My first and most difficult problem was to bring together what seemed to be two unfriendly mediums. In order to work toward plastic harmony and avoid unnecessary complications, I started with a design vertical in form and content. The carving was done directly while keeping in mind the union of mosaic to follow. As I carved, I stopped periodically to place the tesserae along the outline of the figure to formulate the background: the moment I placed the crisp glass mosaic against the softer grain of the wood, the wood seemed to lose its personality. Despite the various color harmonies I tried, the mosaic dominated the sculpture. It became obvious that, in this type of bas-relief, the placement of mosaic tesserae flat on the surface emphasized the aggressive character of the glass and set up a conflict with the more docile wood. After much experimentation, I tried recessing the mosaic by carving channels, or setting beds, around the figure. This was the answer. It enabled me to place the tesserae flush with the background surface of the wood, thus equalizing wood and glass. To contrast the wood surface with the lighter-toned mosaic, I dissolved shoe polish in turpentine and brushed it onto the surface, quickly wiping off the excess with a clean rag. The grain of the wood appeared strong, and the mosaic took the role necessary to this particular union. A great deal of experimentation will have to be done in this field before all the exciting possibilities will be understood and applied.

139

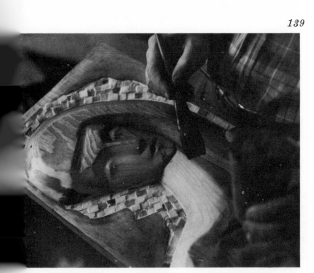

140

141

142

Many people have wondered why the ancient world combined color and form with such ease, while today, the majority of sculptors prefer either monochromatic forms or geometric constructions in primary colors. Other than recent experimental exceptions*, from the Renaissance period on down, sculptors have avoided color. The *mosaic-technique* of assembling works of art is no different today than in the past, and yet most sculptors in our time select materials and develop forms that preclude the use of color.

An important re-evaluation of the past has occurred during the last few years and is initiating a return to basic concepts. Sahl Swarz, well-known American sculptor, recently said: "Our own time is notable for its lack of chromatics in sculpture, mainly due to the difficulty in achieving an integrated feeling between color and form. But in mosaics, the glass pieces are

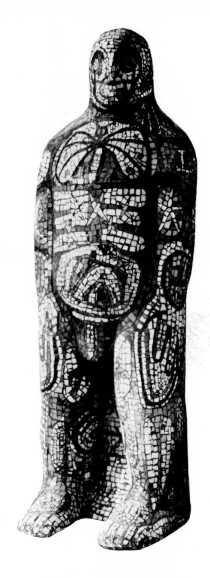

143

141. "Potsherds," bas-relief mosaic in brass, pressed glass, and
ceramic, by sculptor Ted Egri
of Taos, New Mexico.

142. "Crucifix," stained glass
and welded iron, by Ted Egri.

143. "Tattooed Man," a three-
dimensional mosaic sculpture
built up with magnesite super-
imposed over an armature of
pipe and wire, by mosaicist Ray
Rice of San Francisco.

144. "Self-portrait," mosaic
composed of chips of natural
colored woods, by sculptor
Charles Schlein of Los Angeles,
California.

144

the form itself, instead of a superficial embel-
lishment. The surface, due to the hand cutting
of the glass, is alive; it vibrates with diverse
reflections at all angles. Color areas can be naturally modified for complementary relationships by mixing the colors to take advantage of
the pointillistic effect of the medium. In other
words, the colors are not solid; they are made
up of endless fragments with cement between,
so that their spacing and prominence can also
be varied. This adds up to an unusual oppor-
tunity for pleasing manipulation."†

Architects, sculptors, artists, and designers
are becoming concerned with a reintegration of
all the arts in our time, and mosaic (as one of
the most complete organic methods of using
color ever developed by man) has already
earned the right to lead the way.

†From "Sahl Swarz makes a new approach to an ancient
art," *American Artist*, January, 1955.

Bas-relief Mosaics in Cast Concrete

145

146

147

148

149

150

Making poured concrete bas-reliefs in mosaic requires building molds in wood and executing the mosaic within the molds before casting. The process of casting includes painting the mold with a releasing agent (145), cutting and laying in reinforcing wire (146), testing size of heavier galvanized reinforcing bars (147), accurately weighing the cement mix proportions (148), adding metallic oxide coloring (149) and water for mixing (150), shoveling (151) and spreading this colored grout mixture over entire surface by carefully brushing on (152 and 153), putting in the reinforcing grid and covering with a second layer of uncolored cement (154), lining up the attachment bolts (155), and completing pouring and leveling the panels in production line manner (156). The final result is at left (COLOR PLATE V), now standing in Eden Memorial Park, San Fernando, California. Subject is symbols of twelve ancient tribes of Israel. Designed and executed by Joseph Young; William Allen, AIA, Architect. A variation on this theme was also created by the artist for Shalom Memorial Park, Palatine, Illinois, in 1961, where the individual panels were arranged in a much different manner for a special structure designed by Philip Johnson, AIA.

151

152

153

154

155

156

Tilt-up Construction of Mosaics

Tilt-up construction with mosaic is one of the most recent technological advances in contemporary screen-wall construction. In this group of photos the technique is shown as one of the practical methods worked out to cover entire skyscrapers with glass mosaic. This new multi-storied building located on the corner of Wilshire Boulevard and Flower Street in downtown Los Angeles was designed by Victor Gruen & Associates of Beverly Hills. The random medley of dark blue ¾-inch-square tesserae was used in combination with aluminum vertical fins to create a maintenance-free building. This technique is a logical descendant of the prefabricated slab technique first employed on a large scale by construction firms using the Mosai system and by the artist-architect Juan O'Gorman of Mexico City. Presently, experiments are also being conducted with the lift-slab technique and the pre-stressed methods. It is in these particular areas that the mosaic field has grown into a multi-million dollar industry.

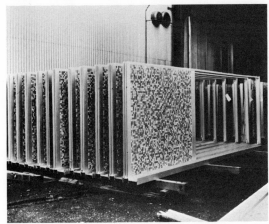

157

158

159

160

Combining Mosaics with Granite

The development of a fresh direction in art integrated with architecture is generally based on a firm knowledge of historical precedents. In the case of the 80 by 20-foot granite and mosaic bas-relief recently completed for the main exterior auditorium wall of the new Los Angeles County Hall of Records, the artist, Joseph Young, found inspiration in the famed Colosseum of ancient Rome. In 1959 the Hall of Records mural project was initiated by the offices of architects Richard J. Neutra, FAIA, and Robert Alexander, FAIA. During the first phase, Young served as consultant, evolving the theme and building the scale models which were approved by the total architectural team of Herman Light, John Rex, Douglas Honnald and James Friend, all members of the American Institute of Architects. The bas-relief, completed in 1962, is an aerial, topographical map that symbolically interprets the water sources and land formation in the County of Los Angeles. Reservoirs were created with bronze cups through which water flows down the mosaic channels into a reflection pool at the base of the map. Lights set in the bottom of the pool create a many-faceted reflection on the granite walls at night. As in the ancient Colosseum of Rome, the main form was designed of concrete, to which the granite and mosaic veneers were attached.

Above condensed from article by Betje Howell, *Creative Crafts*, 1962.

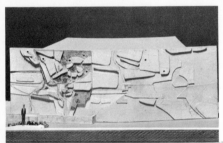

162

163

164

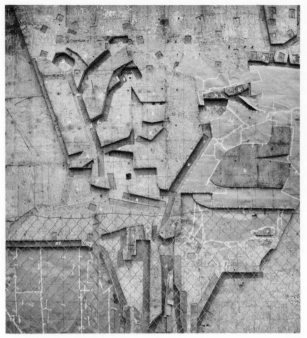

165

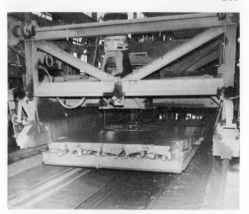

166

167

Working from his scale model (162), the artist laid out a full-scale cartoon which was so large that over-all viewing was made possible only by hanging it on the end wall of a handball court (163). Next, a wood and styro-foam mold was built to provide for pouring the entire wall in concrete after the reinforcing rods were set into place (164). After stripping the mold, the exposed concrete bas-relief (165) was sand blasted, and remeas-ured to make templates for the Minnesota Granite Industries in Delano, Minnesota. There, the granite was slab cut (166), pol-ished (167), and detail cut by hand (168) according to the templates. At the site the artist coordinated the installation with master granite setters (169), ascertaining that the vertical planes of the building were ac-curately repeated by the use of the unique vertical brick pattern to fill the background area around the map. A mosaic effect in this area was achieved by contrasting split-face granite bricks with those of highly pol-ished surfaces. (Continued on next page.)

168

169

170

The final phase of the three-year project was the design and execution of the mosaic portions to represent the Pacific Ocean and main waterways in the county. This was done over a three-month period at the artist's workshop with the assistance of his personally trained apprentices (170). The prefabricated mosaic sections were next laid out at the site (171) and final corrections in color and dimensions made before the three day installation process performed by the Selectile Company of Los Angeles. (See also color Frontispiece.)

171

172

173

The completed Hall of Records mural for the County of Los Angeles represents the second major mural commission completed by Joseph Young for the Los Angeles Civic Center; the first being the cantilevered mosaic mural for the main lobby of the City of Los Angeles Police Facilities Building, completed in 1955 (see page 51), which also initiated a new direction in the use of contemporary mosaics for architecture.

174

174. "White on White," pebble and sand mosaic by Frances Simches. Photo Craft Horizons, July/August, 1960.

Sand Casting Pebble Mosaics

Among the many talented woman mosaicists working today, Jean Johanson of Seattle, Washington, is among the foremost in the use of sand-cast pebble mosaics. Among her most interesting commissions to date are a wall panel for the rectory of the Holy Family Church in Kirland, Washington, and a large mosaic of polished beach pebbles and marble chips for the Broadmoor Golf Club in Seattle. The following description is an adaptation of her technique of working as originally delivered in a paper at the 1961 National American Craftsmen's Council convention in Seattle.

Make a full-scale color cartoon on heavy wrapping paper. To make an edge for the casting, build an accurately squared and leveled frame of the same exterior dimensions as the cartoon, using 2 x 4-inch grade A lumber on edge to get an unwarped 4-inch depth to the frame and being careful to reinforce the exterior of each corner with an angle iron bracket. Should you want the exterior edges also to act as the frame for the mosaic, have a

welder use stainless steel to make the frame and connect the rear of the frame with reinforcing bars welded into position.

After checking the dimensions of the frame by placing the cartoon inside it, place the wood or metal frame down on a sturdy work table or smooth floor covered with a sheet of seamless plastic stretched tight. On the inside of the frame all around scribe a line ½ inch from the bottom to which the sand should come when the pebbles are in place ready to cast. In the frame build a bed of damp, pre-washed fine sand (No. 30 Del Monte) mixed with a small quantity of molasses, which keeps the sand from drying out too fast.

With a template made of wood, smooth down the sand to a level of exactly ⅜ inch from the bottom of the frame, being certain not to pack the sand. Next, cut up the cartoon into the pieces that follow the design, laying one piece at a time into the frame face down on the sand. Along the sides or seams of each new piece scribe the sand lightly with a pencil or stick, thus, unit-by-unit, transferring the outlines of the cartoon to the sand. Upon completing the transfer of the design, reassemble the cartoon pieces with masking tape for future reference while working. Now the rocks and pebbles are ready to go into the sand, first laid on gently and then pressed in so that they are still high enough out of the sand for the cement to have an undercut surface to grip.

When the entire design has been laid out in stones or pebbles, lightly spray the surface with a small amount of water to firm up the sand before casting and to prevent the concrete from drawing out the moisture. Cover the entire frame with a sheet of plastic to prevent dehydration while mixing the concrete. Using a mortar box and hoe, mix a stiff mixture of cement using 2 parts of washed fine sand to 1 part cement, adding to the water 1 per cent of an additive called Plastiment. This additive (which comes under many brand names) slows the setting time, making the concrete more plastic in handling and denser when hardening.

If a colored cement is preferred, then add 3 per cent of the metallic oxide color desired. For an even distribution of the cement, remove the protective plastic sheet from the back of the frame and slowly screen on the cement mixture into the frame through a ¼-inch metal mesh screen. This first layer (the only one to be colored, if preferred) is laid on about ½ inch thick, with great care devoted to getting it even over the whole surface, including the corners and edges. With the first slight stiffening of the concrete, use a wide board and rubber mallet to tamp this surface, first lightly and then increasingly hard. Next, galvanized wire mesh is cut slightly smaller than the inside of the frame and laid on this surface.

The second and final layer of uncolored concrete is screened in to fill up the frame, bonding in the reinforcing mesh. Hooks, expansion bolts, or the sleeves of threaded bolts are set in and connected to the mesh as required while the cement is still plastic; then the entire surface is tamped down again to conform to a 2-inch thickness throughout the frame. Give this back surface a final light spray of water and cover with transparent plastic to slow dehydration during the curing. When the concrete has cured for 24 hours, remove plastic sheets, turn over panel (knock off wood frame only), and wash the surface with a hose. Use a stiff brush to remove any remaining sand; after drying, the surface is ready for waterproofing with silicone sealer. This surface is suitable for walks as well as murals. Avoid caustic soaps or detergents for maintenance.

175

176

177

Through the wars and conquests of ancient times, the Greek and Roman artisans (178) carried the art of making floor mosaics throughout the world. Today, we can see the lovely banded mosaic pavements of Rio de Janeiro (177), contemporary Cosmati work in St. Bartholomew's Church in New York (179) created by V. Foscato, magnificent 5th-century marble mosaics uncovered at Tel Shikmona, Israel (180), a rubble random quarry-tile floor for a modern patio (181), and an occasional glass mosaic floor emblem, like this example done by the author for the new Texaco Building in Los Angeles (182). Many craftsmen have discovered that mosaic floors are literally permanent carpets in their homes and are attractive in the living areas as well as the kitchen and bathroom.

178

179

180

181

182

Mosaics As A Durable Floor Surface

One of the principal reasons for the survival of the floor mosaics of ancient times is a law of ancient Rome that invoked the death penalty if lime less than eight years old was sold for making cement. Today whenever marble mosaic floors are to be installed the concrete foundation floor should be left 2 inches below the finished floor. Over this is placed an underbed of mortar composed of 1 part cement and 3 parts sand, leveled off 1 inch below the finished floor. Next, the setting coat (composed of 1 part Portland cement, 2 parts sand, and a sufficient quantity of lime to make the mortar plastic) should be spread and leveled. The mosaic tesserae should be embedded into this setting coat. Press and tamp them into the mortar until they are firmly positioned. When the mortar is set, remove the paper from the surface and fill the joints with grout. After the floor has firmly set, the whole area can be polished with a terrazzo machine. To set glass mosaic, use a mixture of 1 part Portland cement, 1 part lime putty, and 3 parts clean, sharp sand. The scratch coat for glass mosaic should be given a fine cross scratch, leaving an even thickness of ¾ inch to receive the mosaic work.

Portions of the above were adapted from specifications developed by the National Terrazzo Association. The author concurs with their recommendation that in work of this scale professionals be employed to perform the installations.

183

Stained Glass

Artists of today are re-examining the ancient roots of their art, and the fascinating relationship between stained glass and mosaic. As a direct descendant of mosaic, stained glass became one of the world's most magnificent arts, so completely fulfilled that it has tended to repeat itself for hundreds of years. However, the strength of this traditional outlook has not deterred contemporary architectural artists from pioneering in the creative uses of colored glass. No longer is stained glass bound by the medieval laws that dictated a window must be constructed with leading and rods. Today, there are artists Roger Darricarrere, Peter Ostuni, Robert Mallary, Sam Kaner, Jeanne Reynal, Don Charles Norris, Emile Norman, and many others who are employing the mosaic technique to find new structural means to create transparent and translucent planes that will fill the needs of contemporary architecture.

The photos on this page show how a professional artist-craftsman, Roger Darricarrere, uses the mosaic technique to assemble his structural stained-glass windows in concrete. The chunks of colored glass, made by the artist with equipment of his own design, are 1 to 3 inches thick, capable of remarkable prismatic effect when chipped by hammer (183). Instead of employing traditional leading, Darricarrere embeds the glass in steel-reinforced concrete joints from ¼ inch to 10 inches wide according to the design desired (184). High lights are obtained by varying the thickness of the glass and cement.

184

Robert Mallary fractures the stained glass with a hammer to obtain fortuitous patterns (185) which are then laid, often in many layers, onto a transparent sheet of plexiglas, resting on a special glass-topped worktable lighted from below. In order to control the frosting of the plastic, various transparent powdered materials were sifted onto the surface (186), before and after the plastic was poured (187). The plastic, which can be colored and/or textured before it is poured, locks the pieces of fractured glass together by seeping through the layers to the plexiglas base.

187

186

185

In the field of experimental mediums, Robert Mallary's work is well known and admired. Mallary collaborated with artist Dale Owen during 1955 to create a 6 x 37-foot translucent mosaic mural of stained glass and plastic for the Escoffier Room of the new Beverly Hilton Hotel in Beverly Hills.

The use of both sharp and blurred edges is one of the special features of Mallary's technique, which relates it to painting as well as stained glass and mosaic. In describing his own work, Mallary recently wrote: "Luminous color and light, and what might be called *light-textures* offer great possibilities, and I often think of my work as simply an extension of stained glass and mosaic. While I do think that technical experimentation alone is not enough justification for a work of art, I do believe that the excitement of research can lead to good art. Indeed, the value of a new medium can only be demonstrated by the quality of the work which emerges from it."

"The Seven Days of the Week," a 6 x 37-foot translucent mosaic mural made of stained glass and plastic, designed and executed by Robert Mallary and Dale Owens in 1954-55 for the Beverly Hilton Hotel, Beverly Hills, California. Welton Becket FAIA & Associates, Architects.

188

189.

189. *Dick Seeger, an artist in plastics from Phoenix, Arizona, developed this original use of transparent mosaics for the fur department of Goldwater's Park Central department store. Welton Becket, FAIA, of Los Angeles was the architect.*

190. *Sam Kaner, originally from New York and now living in Copenhagen, has continued with his experiments in translucent mosaics. This example used Venetian glass mounted on plexiglas.*

191. *Travelers passing through American Airlines terminal at the New York International Airport have long admired the block-long stained glass window designed by Robert Sowers of New York. Done in a mosaic technique, the windows are very effective day and night.*

192. *The more humble varieties of plastics so often found today in homes lend themselves to a spirited use. Here an outdoor screen for a contemporary home in Los Angeles serves a multipurpose in screening the powder room from the entranceway while lighting the driveway at night. Water slides down the surface to recirculate the reflection pool. Designed and executed by Joseph Young.*

193. *Peter Ostuni of New York has won a wide reputation for his transparent and translucent panels in glass and plastics that remind one of mosaics. The Prudential Life Insurance offices in New York have this reception area panel.*

190.

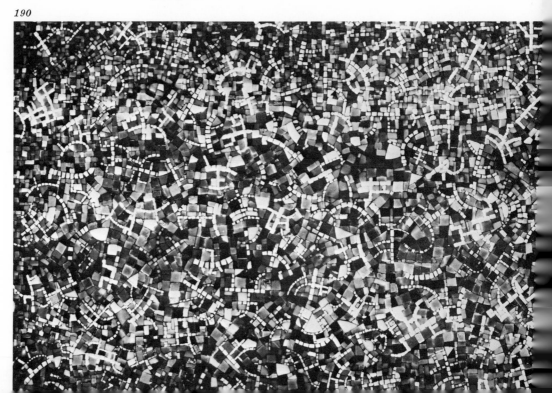

191

193

192

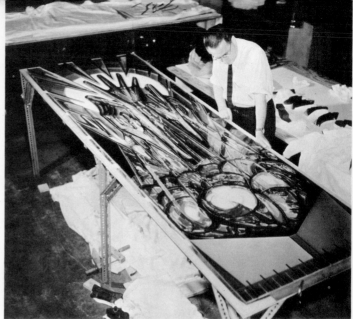

194. *Another important investigator in the realm of plastics is the noted muralist Abraham Joel Tobias of New York. Using the plastics factory as his temporary studio, artist Tobias undertook this recent commission by working directly with the materials.*

195. *Edge-cementing an element of the mural to the white translucent Plexiglas base plate, Tobias built up layers of plastic to produce subtle color variations and three-dimensional effects. The raised ribs are part of the design, and not for mechanical reasons as in stained glass construction.*

196. *The completed murals for the main entrance of the new Brooklyn Polytechnic Institute Building in New York combine the best design attributes of plastics and stained glass through the mosaic technique.*

COLOR PLATE VI. *One of the most promising innovations in combining mosaic with plastic has been the rapid evolution of lighting fixtures made with mosaic. The cylinders are generally available through local suppliers of plastics and transparent adhesives are used to apply the glass.*

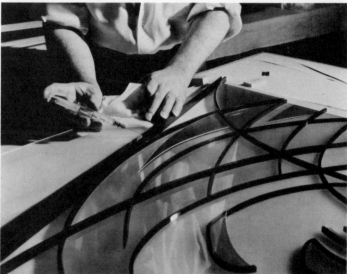

195

196

197

198

EMILE

NORMAN

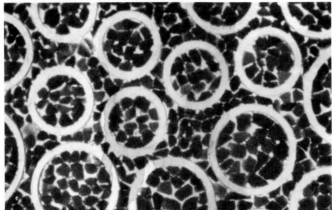

199

200

Mosaics In Plastics

Emile Norman of Big Sur, California, has developed a medium which he calls "endomosaic." In technique it consists of laying a lightly textured sheet of Plexiglas, textured side down, over a light table and gluing the tesserae into place with a transparent adhesive. Bits of metal, parchment, felt, linen, silk, natural foliage and thinly sliced vegetable matter, shells and sea life, plus any of 180 colors of stained glass may be used flat or on edge or crushed and sieved. Fastened down, the tesserae are cast in liquid plastic to hold them permanently in position and the second sheet of Plexiglas is bonded on. Recently Emile Norman completed a 40 x 48-foot window for the Masonic Memorial Temple in San Francisco (201). Depicting the history of California Masonry, the series of 6 x 8-foot endomosaic panels were designed to face south for maximum light. Details on this page are from the finished window, opposite.

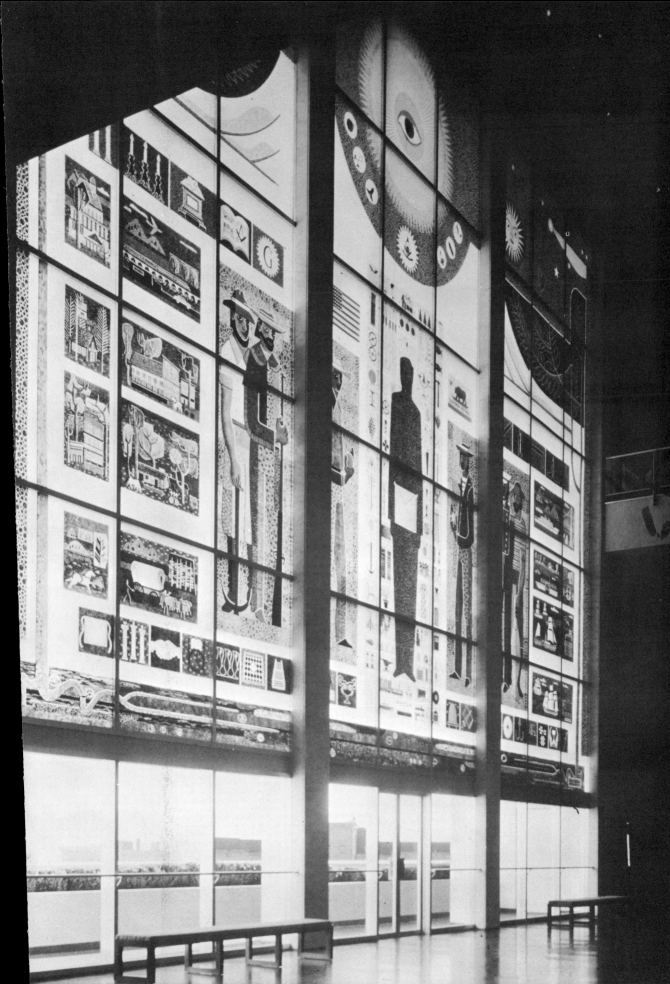

202 COLORED SAND

From the molecular use of silicates the next step-up in tesserae size is sand. Here is an example of the Work of Leonora Cetone of Los Angeles, who adheres colored sands to Masonite with Wilhold glue to make sand mosaics.

202

203

203 TERRAZZO MOSAICS

Few American families have been more active in the field of mosaics than the Bruton sisters of California. All three have done mosaics in rock and glass. Here is an example of Margaret's work in terrazzo for the Standard Federal Savings & Loan Association of Los Angeles; Welton Becket FAIA & Associates, Architects.

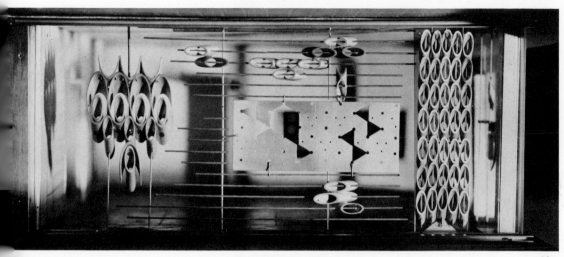

204 METALLIC SCREENS

*The potentialities of metal
sheets, rods, and extruded shapes
assembled in a mosaic-technique
are being explored by many artists today. Muralist Robert Lep-
per of the Carnegie Institute of
Technology, Pittsburgh, carried
out this particular project in
conjunction with Alcoa. Notable
work in this field is also being
done by Harry Bertoia and
Mary Callery of New York.*

205 THREAD MOSAICS

*Today, the art of making tapes-
tries is no longer restricted to
the loom, as exemplified by this
imaginative thread mosaic, "The
Nativity," by Albert J. Kramer
of Los Angeles. Other artists
who are doing outstanding work
in this field include Everett K.
Sturgeon of New York, and
John Smith of Los Angeles.*

205

MOSAICS AS A COMMUNITY ART FORM

Mosaic Murals for Public Buildings

Marble mosaic mural, side entrance to La Rinascente department store, Milan, Italy, designed by Massimo Campigli; executed by Giovanetti of Rome; Carlo Pagano, Architect, 1950.

206

Ceramic tile mosaic mural, Pershing Municipal Auditorium, Lincoln, Nebraska, designed by Leonard Thiessen and Bill J. Hammon in collaboration with Harry J. Macke, Art Director of Cambridge Tile Company, Cincinnati, Ohio, who carried out prefabrication. Architects: Davis, Wilson, Craig, Hazen, Robinson, Schaumberg & Freeman, 1957.

207

208

Italian glass mosaic mural, 17 x 51 feet, main lobby AFL-CIO Building, Washington, D.C., designed by Lumen Martin Winter, NSMP, executed by BMPIU No. 2 members with Ravenna Mosaic Company, St. Louis, Missouri, 1956.

209

Seven mosaic panels for main dining room of S.S. President Coolidge, American President Lines, designed and executed by John Smith, 1956.

210

1,200 square foot Byzantine glass mosaic mural, lobby of 711 Third Avenue, New York, designed by Hans Hofmann, executed by V. Foscato, William Lescaze, Architect, 1956.

"Symbols of Ancient Commerce," marble mosaic for Commerce Building, Madison, Wisconsin, by James Watrous, 1957.

211

212

Mosaic mural in plaster, Calderone Theatre, Hempstead, Long Island, New York, designed by Max Spivak; executed by V. Foscato; William Lescaze, Architect.

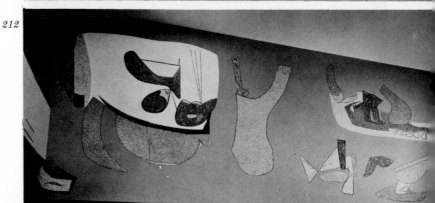

Unglazed ceramic tile mosaic designed by Ada Korsakaite, Leighton's, Fifth Avenue, New York; Victor Gruen and Associates, AIA, Architects, 1956.

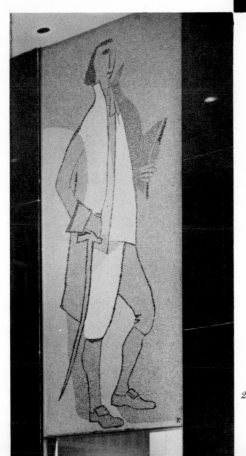

213

214

Marble mosaic mural, exterior entrance to Wasson's Recreation Center, Winnipeg, Canada, designed by George Swinton; Charles Faurer, Architect, 1956.

Glass mosaic mural integrated into rock screen of lava, Canlis Broiler Restaurant, Hawaii, designed by Ben Norris; executed by Bumpei Akaji; Wimberly & Cook, AIA, Architects, 1956.

215

216. "Prehistoric Forms," broken and cut tiles in prefabricated panels, 30 by 10 feet, designed and executed by Antony Hollaway, A.R.C.A., for the Brandon Estate Clubroom, London County Council, London, 1960.

217. "Art of Communication," smalti mosaic in brass frames, for exterior facade of radio station in Canada by Lionel Thomas of University of British Columbia, Vancouver, British Columbia, 1959.

218. "New York Skyline," smalti mosaic panel, 4 x 8 feet, designed and executed for entrance to stock exchange offices in Santa Barbara, California, by Joseph Young, 1959.

219. East front panel for County Power Building, Sacramento, California, by Wayne Thiebaud of Sacramento. Venetian glass mosaic, prefabricated in Italy.

220. Milwaukee County War Memorial mosaic mural designed by Edmund Lewandowski, completed in 1959. Eero Saarinen, Architect.

221. Exterior entrance to 111 West 40th Street in New York, designed by Max Spivak of New York. Executed in Byzantine smalti, approximately 500 square feet. Kahn & Jacobs, AIA, Architects.

217

218

219

220

221

222

223

Mosaics, once an art limited to royal patronage, today has become a medium many architects have found exceptionally beautiful to incorporate when planning buildings for corporate clients. In Austin, Texas, the architectural firm of Brooks & Barr, A.I.A., commissioned Paul Hatgil and Michael Frary to do an 8 x 10-foot entrance-way mural titled "Panorama" (222) for Mrs. Lyndon B. Johnson. Jerome and Evelyn Ackerman of Los Angeles, California, worked with architect Sherril Broudy to design an attractive vertical accent to an apartment house (223). In New York's Rockefeller Center the Manufacturer's Trust has a horizontal translucent mosaic (224) designed by Gyorgy Kepes, famed author

224

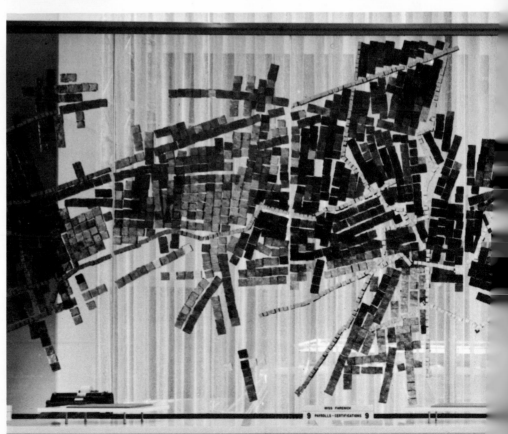

and educator from the Massachusetts Institute of Technology in Cambridge, Massachusetts. Recently, artist Kepes completed a large mosaic mural for the main lobby of the new Prudential Life Insurance building in Los Angeles, which was commissioned by Welton Becket, F.A.I.A., and Associates. Other murals that have attracted international attention are in New York at 2 Broadway, by Lee Krasner and Ronald Stein (225); in Seattle on the front of the new Power and Light Building by Jean Beall (227); and in Cairo, Egypt, where Herb Rosenthal of Los Angeles planned the enormous exterior facade of the Nile Hilton for Welton Becket, FAIA, and Associates (226).

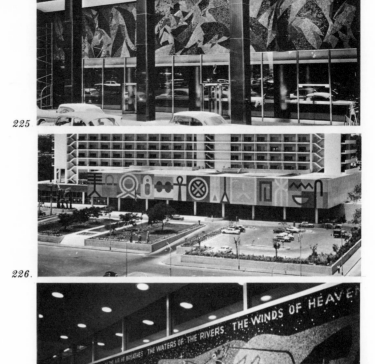

225

226.

227.

228

228. "Education," 24 by 8-foot Byzantine mosaic mural by Sister Augusta for main entrance to Seton High School, Cincinnati, Ohio, 1960. The city of Cincinnati is also noted for a series of monumental mosaics completed for the main railway terminal over 25 years ago.

229

229. "Children at Study," 16 by 20-foot mosaic mural, by Jack and Margot Stewart for Public School 28 in New York City, 1959. Maurice Courland & Son, architects-Engineers. Nahama Courland, interior designer.

230

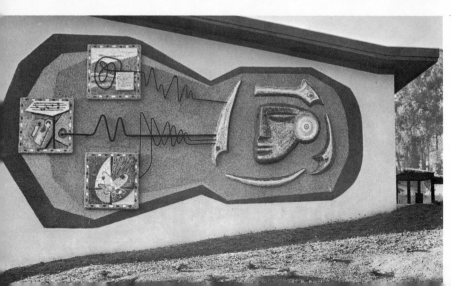

230. "Communication," 20 x 9-foot bas-relief Byzantine mosaic mural for exterior auditorium wall of Sophia College of Holy Names, Oakland, California, by Louisa Jenkins of Big Sur, California, 1959.

231

The exciting collaborative efforts in recent years by architects and artists have demonstrated that art in architecture is fundamental to building for education. At the 1960 opening convocation of the University of South Florida in Tampa, two dramatic mosaic murals by Joe Testa-Secca were dedicated. Architect Mark Hampton also commissioned artist Testa-Secca to create bas-reliefs for the new chemistry buildings.

Detail of tile mosaic murals, El Centro Escolar Independencia, Morelia, Mexico, designed, executed, and installed by Robert Hansen, 1953.

232

233

234

"Greek Chorus" mosaic mural, Penthouse Theatre, University of Washington, Seattle, designed and executed by Jean Beall, 1955.

Italian glass mosaic mural, Allen-Bradley Building, Milwaukee, Wisconsin, designed by Edmund Lewandowski; executed in Venice, Italy, 1957.

Public libraries are civic institutions of learning where mosaics are particularly appropriate when they are incorporated into the architecture. Some outstanding examples are a horizontal band of symbols designed by Edmund Lewandowski for the Everett Library in Milwaukee (235); the origin and evolution of the alphabet designed and executed by Lionel and Patricia Thomas for the Vancouver Public Library in British Columbia (236); and a bold abstract symbolizing an open book for the Oakland Public Library by Robert Holdeman of San Francisco (237). Lewandowski employed Byzantine smalti throughout his mural while the Thomases and Holden used a combination of Venetian and Byzantine glass. Lionel Thomas is considered one of Canada's most outstanding mosaic muralists at work today.

236

237

Ecclesiastical Work

238

239

Two panels from a "Stations of the Cross" series designed and executed in mosaic by Louisa Jenkins of Big Sur, California for the Mt. Angel Abbey in Oregon, 1953.

The "Star of David" and the "Menorah", two symbolic panels for a Jewish Temple, designed and executed by Ada Korsakaite in unglazed ceramic tile.

240

241

242

In Sioux Falls, South Dakota, architect Harold Spitznagel, A.I.A., collaborated with Palmer Eide of Augustana College to evolve a contemporary interpretation of traditional symbols (242) for a new Protestant church in that area. Conrad Schmitt of Milwaukee stressed a vertical concept in his Tree of Life mosaic (243) for the Mother of Perpetual Help Church.

243

COLOR PLATE *VII.*

Byzantine glass mosaic mural,
9 by 16 feet for main entrance
to the Don Bosco Technical
High School, South San Gabriel,

California, designed and exe-
cuted by Joseph L. Young;
Barker & Ott, A.I.A., architects,
1956.

Mosaic mural for main entrance foyer of Temple Emanuel, Beverly Hills, California, designed and executed by Joseph L. Young. First major mosaic for sanctuary area of Jewish temple since Biblical times. Architect, Sidney Eisenshtat, A.I.A.

244

245

246

The enormous surge in contemporary church building throughout the world has helped restore mosaic to its ancient position as an ideal medium for ecclesiastic work. The breadth of this construction activity has encouraged a healthy diversity of style and technique. For example, Harold Haydon, who teaches on the art faculty of the University of Chicago, elected to use Byzantine Glass mosaic for a Jewish Temple commission (244); Diederich Kortlang in Puerto Rico used marble tesserae to create a stolid Angel (245); in illustration 246 an impressionistic technique was employed in the head of Christ; Rambush of New York used an archeological style for the Shrine Altar they completed for the Byzantine Seminary in Pittsburgh (247); while Miriam Sommerburg, also of New York, created a Menorah triptych in Venetian glass (248).

247

248

249. *Detail of mosaic mural in St. Mary's Church, Berne, Switzerland. Designed by Jordan and executed by Salviati and Company, Venice.*

250. *Byzantine glass mosaic mural for Marquette University, designed by Edmund Lewandowski of Milwaukee. Executed in Venice, 1953.*

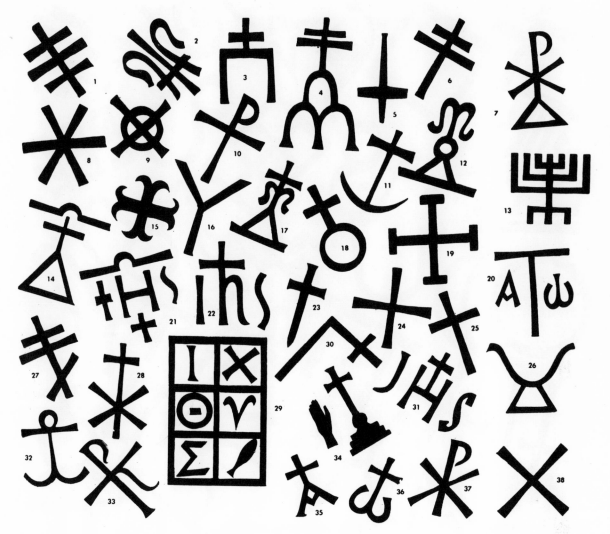

Useful Symbols

1—Eight-ended Russian Ortho-
dox cross. 2—Lily. 3—Cross
over arch. 4—Cross of Lorraine
on three hills. 5—St. Peter's
cross. 6—Cross of Lorraine. 7—
Holy Trinity. 8—Chrismon. 9—
Denotes church has been conse-
crated. 10—Ansated cross. 11—
Christ born of Mary. 12—Holy
Trinity. 13—Symbol of Old Testament, seven branched candle-
stick. 14—Three Persons of the
Trinity. 15—Cross moline. 16—
Fork cross, thieve's cross. 17—
Holy Trinity. 18—Orb of the
world. 19—Cross potent. 20—
Tau cross with Alpha and
Omega. 21—Monogram of Jesus
denoting redemption, or the
Holy Ghost. 22—Monogram of
Christ. 23—Cross Patée Fitchée.
24—Greek cross. 25—Latin
cross. 26—Symbol of faith. 27—
Russian cross. 28—Cross and
Chrismon. 29—The letters form-
ing the word "fish" in Greek are
the initial letters of five Greek
words meaning "Jesus Christ,
Son of God, Savior." 30—Chev-
ron cross. 31—Monogram of
Jesus. 32—Anchor cross. 33—
Chrismon. 34—Manus Deus. 35
—Alpha. 36—Omega. 37—Chris-
mon. 38—St. Andrew's cross.

USEFUL SYMBOLS (continued)

1—Poisonous. 2—Day. 3—Pot-hanger. 4—Cruciform. 5—The wave. 6—Very poisonous, deadly. 7—The moon in ascending node. 8—Lily of Cleves. 9—Fork. 10—Leo, the Lion: July. 11—Water. 12—Three crowns. 13—Libra. 14—Summer. 15—Aquarius, the Water Bearer: January. 16—Taurus, the Bull: April. 17—Sunday. 18—Monday. 19—Winter. 20—Vesta. 21—Bush. 22—Scorpio, the Scorpion: October. 23—Autumn. 24—Pernicious, suspect. 25—Pisces, the Fishes: February. 26—Saturday. 27—Virgo, the Virgin: August. 28—Mercury. 29—Mars. 30—Thursday. 31—Sagittarius, the Archer: November. 32—Neptune. 33—Evening. 34—Capricornus, the Goat. 35—Gemini, the Twins: May. 36—Aries, the Ram: March. 37—Spring. 38—Cancer, the Crab: June. 39—Venus. 40—Pallas. 41—Ceres.

252

100

OUTSTANDING MOSAICISTS

Without question, one of the most significant mosaicists in our time is Gino Severini, now living in Paris. If his only accomplishment rested upon creating the link between the color theories of Impressionism and the form concepts developed by the Cubists, this alone would be a record of a brilliant career. However, Gino Severini went on to demonstrate that the future of modern art depends entirely upon the artists willing to meet the architectural needs of our time.

SANFORD ROTH   *253*

Gino Severini

While in Rome in 1901, Gino Severini met Boccioni, who was later to become the leader of Futurism. In 1906 he moved to Paris and worked alongside Braque, Picasso, Dufy, Utrillo, Valadon, and poets Max Jacob and Apollinaire. During this period his paintings were inspired by Seurat. As one of the signers of the Futurist manifesto, he arranged the meeting between the Futurists and the Cubists, and went on to fulfill his early promise by painting "Pan-Pan at the Monico," the acknowledged masterpiece of Futurism. After the Cubists saw Severini's paintings in the first Futurist exhibition held at the Bernheim-Jeune Gallery in 1910, many of them abandoned their monochromatic approach to return to color.

True to his early Italian influence, Severini gravitated toward the direction being developed by Leger, Metzinger, and Gleizes. This concern with the monumental found expression in a series of frescoes executed for the Montegufoni Castle near Florence, in 1922. In the many productive years that followed, he painted frescoes and executed mosaics for churches in Semsales, LaRoche, Fribourg, and Lausanne. In addition, Severini executed many notable mosaics in Italy and France for public buildings, and is highly regarded as one of the rare

artists who spent his life insisting upon the essential sense of permanency that must return to art.

Gino Severini, as the major international leader in the art of mosaic today, has written a magnificent volume of memoirs, and has lectured on the art of mosaic throughout Europe. The following quotes, translated by Beulah Roth of Los Angeles, are excerpts from his correspondence with the author, and from his address, "Mosaics and the Art of Murals in Ancient and Modern Times," which he delivered at a conference in Ravenna, Italy, in June, 1952, under the auspices of The Society for the Friends of Art.

"In each form of expression, but especially in mosaics, design and technique are *inseparable*. Technique reveals what is deepest in man; the eternal need to create something with his hands. A need which is a will, a hunger. In the mosaicist's hands everything takes life, from the hammers and chisels to the stones and enamels. They become vibrant and impatient as a ballet dancer waiting to go on stage.

"It is necessary for there to be an accord between painting and architecture. It implies not only a conception of space but a clear understanding of chromatic values so as not to destroy with color what was constructed with line. If I have so much interest, and I might add so much love, for that marvelous form of art, mosaics, it is because I have so much respect for the materials which characterize it. Mosaic can be a powerful force in reintroducing order, clarity and purity into Art. It can also bring to Art a sense of reality which the modern world with its antagonists can no longer do.

"Basically, the artist does not want to be understood. Often, he suffers most from being understood. What he most desires is to last through the ages. The mosaicist is surrounded by an atmosphere of contradiction, and like all other artists he has to live in it and work in it. I believe that even the exigencies of a mosaicist's career should by no means prevent him from participating in the hope of other artists. Such associations will help him to choose the direction which suits him best and help protect him from the seduction of extremist thought."

254

255

Detail from mosaic mural, Church of St. Pierre, Fribourg, Switzerland.

256

Juan O'Gorman

MOSAICS — MEXICO — O'GORMAN
by Esther McCoy

It is not by chance that the integration of mosaics into architecture in our time was first achieved on a monumental scale in Mexico. Juan O'Gorman's library at University City, in which an acre of exterior walls is entirely covered with Mexico's history visualized in millions of stones gathered from many states of the Republic, occurred not only by the happy coincidence of O'Gorman's combined gifts as muralist and architect, but is the result of Mexico's traditional love of completed buildings. Throughout its history, Mexico has used its walls for the expression of artistic feelings, making art inseparable from architecture.

Juan O'Gorman prepared his mosaics in slabs, one meter square, and applied them to the superstructure of the library much in the same spirit that the sculptured blocks of limestone were used to form continuous ornament in the Maya temples. By permitting the movement of his narrative to flow freely over the face of the walls, breaking through its grid form, he arrives at a kind of history writing which takes into account the movement of the observer.

"In working out the composition for the four walls of the library," he says, "the first thing was to find a scale of plastic values to fit the building, one which would be correct in size when seen from various points of view, without

257

258

259

Expanding the cartoon (257) to modular units.

over-small detail or over-large figures, which would have destroyed the monumentality of the building. The second thing was to relate the material of each wall to the composition of the four walls so that they would count as one unit plastically and esthetically. In the third place, it was necessary to bring each of the four walls into dynamic symmetry so the total composition would form one geometric structure in three dimensions, while its time dimension was given in the historical theme depicting a different period of Mexico's culture for each wall."

Drawings for the library walls were first made in small scale, then copied in reverse in full scale on heavy paper marked off into square

meters. The cartoon was then cut up and laid on the ground where moulds, also one meter square, were placed over each unit. The stones were then laid on the drawing and the mould filled with an inch of concrete. Steel reinforcing rods with anchor hooks were sunk into the concrete so that the slabs could be attached to a trellis of steel already fixed to the library walls. When the concrete had cured, the paper was stripped away and the stones wire-brushed. Joints between the 4,000 separate slabs were filled with additional concrete after they had been hooked into place.

O'Gorman first tried out natural stone mosaics in his own house in San Angel and later in his house in the Pedregal. In both houses he

Juan O'Gorman and one of his mosaics at his home in the Pedregal.

260

applied the stone directly to a mastic spread on the surface of the walls, floor, or ceiling. It is not by accident, O'Gorman thinks, that mosaics have played a large role in the architecture of fantasy. "Antonio Gaudi used ceramic mosaics as a necessary complement to the baroque forms of his great architecture, and it is evident that without the mosaics he could never have achieved the wonderful snake-like balustrade in the Guell Park at Barcelona, Spain (263), nor the color and texture of the roofs, walls, and pinnacles of his great buildings."

In speaking of his admiration for Fernand Cheval's magic palace of Hauterives, France, and Raymond Isidor's poetic Chateau des Assiettes Cassees (Castle of Broken Plates) in Chartres, O'Gorman says, "These breaths of freshness and pure creation, where the imagination is applied for the expression of freedom, are a wonderful relief in the stagnant academic atmosphere of our pretentious commercial modern times, and reveal the aspiration of liberty of the common people, their love of decorative free expression, which is the beneficial character of the baroque. I use the word baroque because I cannot find a better one to designate the complicated, colorful, and intricate possibilities of an architecture using mosaics, whether on the flat or curved surfaces of walls and ceilings, or as a permanent form to polychrome sculpture.

"The advantage of mosaic over painting is the greater consistency achieved in architecture, because they are built into the architecture. Another advantage is the possibility of their use on the outside of buildings, and this brings us into the realm of color as part of architecture, which in antiquity and up to the Renaissance was always an essential part of the composition."

261

262

263

264

265

International conventions of mosaicists are rare events; the last two were held five years apart. In June, 1959, the Rotary Club of Ravenna, Italy, in cooperation with the Chamber of Commerce, the National Society for Tourism, and the National Museum of Ravenna, invited mosaicists from throughout Europe to attend a three day conclave that included seminars, demonstrations and an exceptional exhibition of contemporary mosaics. The author, who was a guest of the Italian Government and representing America, was invited to screen the film "The World of Mosaic" and deliver an address. The exhibition of mosaics by internationally recognized artists was held at the National Museum and later travelled throughout Europe and the United States. On the next several pages is a selection of these interesting works.

At left (265) the author and the famed Venetian painter, Vedova, attend a banquet honoring Professor Giuseppe Bovini, Inspector of Monuments at Ravenna, as principal organizer of the international mosaic exhibition and convention in 1959 (264). Other distinguished scholars and civic leaders who attended were Marco Vasecchi, Giuseppe Salietti, Giuseppe Medici, Umberto Tupini, Bruno Zevi, Palma Bucarelli, Giulio Carlo Argan, Antonio Manzone, Mario Vistoli and Professor Deluigi. To the right are the works of Mirko (266), Capogrossi (267), Afro (268) and Campigli (269). All of these works were executed under the supervision of Professor Giuseppe Salietti, director of the group of Ravenna mosaicists, with various artisans carrying out the cartoons of the invited artists.

266

267

268

269

271

273

Vedova (270), Gentilini (271), Mathieu (272), Corpora (273), and Saetti (274). The French expressionist, Mathieu, and the Italian architect, Deluigi, were the only two exhibitors to execute their own designs. In the case of both, the work reveals the relevance of Gino Severini's comments (see page 102) at the 1952 International Convention of Mosaicists. Mathieu improvised by manipulating hot strands of glass before they annealed. Just prior to the 1957 exhibition, Saetti, also from Venice, collaborated on a major set of glass-within-glass windows with Venini of Murano.

274

272

275

Birolli (275), Reggiani (276), Guttuso (277), Santomaso (278), Moreni (279) and Paulucci (280). Here the diversity of style among contemporary painters is self-evident. As indicated in the next two pages the problems of relating contemporary painting to mosaics are considerable.

276

277

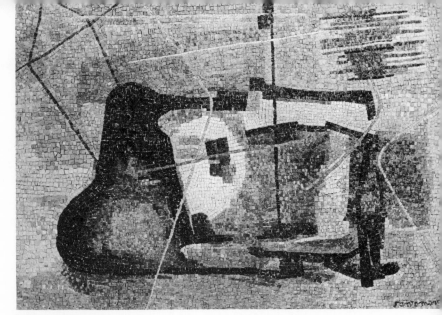

278

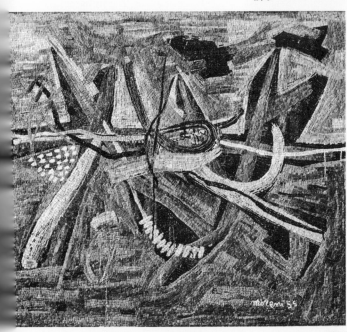

279

280

WHY MOSAICS ARE NOT PAINTING IN GLASS

Mosaics vs. Painting

Today, mosaics are often described by critics as, at best, paintings in glass. Such critics like to cite the renowned Vatican mosaic workshops in Rome where direct copying of oil masterpieces is practiced with technical virtuosity. What such critics fail to mention is the obvious documentary purposes of such copying practices, a policy whereby the great painting masterpieces of the past are preserved for future generations to see. No supporter of today's inflated market in oil paintings likes to admit that Time has a nasty habit of turning oil paintings black with age!

Precedent for the Vatican policy can be found in the famous Alexander the Great mosaic resurrected from the ashes of ancient Pompeii and now permanently on exhibition in the Naples Museum. Historians remind us that the original was a Greek painting and the Pompeian masterpiece is a copy made in marble mosaic. Although small credit is given to the fact that little would be known about ancient painting if mosaic copies had not been made, such documentary efforts by skillful artisans are the thread-bare criteria by which contemporary critics judge mosaics. Many contemporary painters prefer such convenient historical comparisons, since they do seem to show mosaics as being subservient to the art of painting.

Obviously such shortsighted criticism overlooks 800 years of mosaic masterpieces created when the Byzantines ruled the world; the period when mosaics came into their own as an art medium. At the climax of this great era in Ravenna, the mosaicists were considered artists who had progressed beyond painting. Our heritage is their evidence; their belief that glass was the only medium whereby their statement could be made for posterity. Today, with many art schools still emphasizing the post-Renaissance period as a beginning point for their students, the significance of the Byzantine period is much misunderstood. Too few leaders in the arts of today can afford to admit that the Renaissance opened the door to specialization in the arts and from that point on the general movement in the arts has been steadily away from people.

The reawakening of interest in mosaics throughout the world may mean this movement away from people has run its course and art may be ready to again emanate from all the people. Because the tendency of painting to dominate all other mediums is still very strong, such a direction will not necessarily

281

282

283

284

come of itself. This tendency has been strong since the 16th century, the time when painting as a medium became economically geared to consciously swallow up and/or corrupt all other competing mediums. Ceramics, tapestry, and stained glass, like mosaics, all waged losing struggles in the 17th and 18th centuries.

During the 15th century mosaics held an illustrious position among the arts and any objective study of past cultures disproves the contemporary prejudice that easel painting always was or always will be at the top of the aesthetic totem pole. When compared to the much longer history of mosaics or ceramics, the art of painting in oils is a medium that has become senile before it had a chance to get out of its adolescence. Specialization after the Renaissance did push painting into one of the highest forms of plastic expression from the 16th through the 19th centuries; however, just before the turn of this century, men such as Cézanne, Pissarro, Seurat, Renoir and Monet realized that painting was literally expiring from the lack of content that comes from color.

Unfortunately these painters were unaware that the archeologists were discovering Pompeii, and so as artists they found it necessary to invent "Impressionism," the color theories of which were well understood by the Greeks, Romans and Byzantines centuries before. Men of obvious genius expended much talent and energy trying to revitalize a dying technique in the vain hope it would make art aware of the content that comes from color. Such historical mishaps in knowledge have occurred repeatedly in science, but every successful modern art theorist becomes myopic if a parallel is drawn. This very thought defies the current artificial thesis of most critics that

art has no progressive chain of accumulated knowledge. Most artists know better, but today painters such as Amedeo Modigliani (283), Georges Braque (282), Paul Klee (281), and Gauguin (284) are presented by authorities as original thinkers in color. In reality, their principal contribution was to follow the tortuous path established by their predecessors, the Impressionists; that desperate route littered with the artistic bones of individuals, such as Van Gogh, who refused to give up their hunger for a societal image. In other words, the expressionists were, through their art, instinctively trying to go back to the past that preceded the Renaissance, to an age when art was the integrated force projecting images from within the totality of society. Although these early 20th century pioneers attempted to open the door to the contemporary meaning of this past, they did not have the vision to see the next step initiated by Gino Severini (see page 101). Instead, they fathered the present generation of "academic" moderns who have, in turn, strayed still further from the needs of society by giving up the revolt against those forces which converted painting from an art into the manufacturing of aesthetic commodities. Today, the law of supply and demand is still applied to art because painting has elected to stay swift and perishable; a medium well suited to an art without content. For nearly 50 years now painting has advocated a totally intuitive use of color and all this may be invalidated in a few brief years by the rapid return of mosaics; a medium in which 25,000 specific colors can be systematically studied and employed. The majority of people did not discover mosaics through the auspices of museums or galleries and couldn't care less. This same group of people made ceramics into an important addition to American art and they will not be denied their allied interest in mosaics. At the same time, many of the more advanced practitioners of all the reviving mediums are aware they have been categorized as second-class citizens in the arts and have begun to refuse to accept this inferior position. Painting and mosaics have always had elements in common, but they have parted paths once before and are doing so again. In the past, painting dominated in the conflict of interests and purposes, but in our time it will be mosaics that will open the door to equality of the arts. Our democratic times call for participation by all people in the arts and equality of mediums on all levels will be the first sign of artistic maturity.

285

286

287

288

289

290

Portraits in Mosaic

Creating a convincing portrait in mosaic is one of the most demanding challenges in the medium. As in all mosaics of quality, considerable thought and intense study should be devoted to the preparation of a highly detailed cartoon. Every single stone and its placement should contribute toward making a successful total image. In the reproduction above by the author (291), a simplification of the facial planes of *The Prophet* was stressed by the juxtaposition of warm and cool colors. The range of mosaic as a medium readily lends itself to portraits created in any style or manner. The photographic realism of 286 might be compared with the much more contemporary *Harlequin* by Joseph Lasker (287) and the woman's head by Diederich Kortlang (285). Note how the ceramic tile copy of a Holbein portrait (288) as executed by Ada Korsakite for the St. Thomas More Church in Monterey Park, California, has a much different effect from the clean, classical cutting found in the head of Empress Theodora (289) from the 6th-century mosaics at San Vitale in Ravenna, Italy. A broad heroic approach suitable for murals, 290 is an example of a young man's portrait, which is a detail from the facade of Sabaudia's Church in Italy, executed by Salviati and Company of Venice.

292

Shades of Antioch!

In ancient times, the city of Antioch had many pavements in marble mosaic depicting its deities. Recently, mosaic floors were designed for the main entrance to the National Gallery in London. Sir Winston Churchill, Edith Sitwell, and Bertrand Russell are immortalized in portraits that are witty satires on the Victorian virtues of "Wonder," "Curiosity" and "Open Mind." Similar plans were afoot in Hollywood, where a community "beautification" program envisioned mosaic portraits of film stars embedded in the sidewalks of Hollywood Boulevard and Vine Street. Over $300,000 was spent to have 1,507 names of the stars outlined in brass strips within terrazzo. The moral of this story: if the robed citizens of ancient Antioch could stroll upon mosaic representations of *their* gods, why should contemporary man be bashful?

America's 20th Century Folk Art

There seldom has been a word like mosaic (unless it is money) that means so many different things to so many people. Depending upon your personal taste and means, you can find a myriad of things described as mosaic; from a $5.95 "do it yourself mosaic kit" at your local department store to a fourteen thousand eight-hundred and fifty dollar bracelet advertised by Tiffany & Company of New York as a mosaic design.

Just how Tiffany's elegant bracelet, "spirited with Near Eastern splendor," may have been inspired by the type of mosaic broach Cleopatra probably wore for Mark Anthony is not all there is to be told. Like many things, it's the information between that's fascinating. Approximately 5000 years is as far back as the archeologists have been able to find examples of mosaic art. Of course, there are historians who suspect we may one day find mosaics much older, but there are many more people here in America who are more interested to find out why the revival of interest in Mosaics seems to have been born yesterday. Actually it wasn't!

293

294

Since Colonial times America has regarded the fascinating art of making mosaics somewhat the way a timid suitor courts a beautiful woman . . . mostly from afar. Nevertheless, affection grew, as can be seen by the oblique ways the word mosaic entered our language. It was first known either by its Old Testament origins as the Mosaic Law * handed down by Moses, or as pertaining to the ancient art of the Muses. From these Hebrew and Greek origins the word mosaic progressed to descriptive usages.

Farm experts employed the term to describe the virus condition of certain plant diseases; zoologists used the word to indicate the compound-eye characteristic of insects; and aerial topographers found mosaic a word ideally suited to explain the process of assembling terrain photos. But even such a fair daughter of European culture as mosaic, possessed of an ageless beauty sought by kings and empires, had to wait some time before a growing America could overcome its Puritan scepticism of permanence.

*MOSAIC LAW — ancient law of Hebrews, moral and ceremonial, attributed to Moses; contained in Hexateuch, Penta-teuch, and Joshua; also in Ezekiel XI-xlviii, as well as in Scriptures.

295 *296*

BEFORE GRANT TOOK RICHMOND! It took over a century before shy word usages warmed into a proper Victorian declaration of intentions. But today, we are immersed in a fantastic variety of things called mosaic; aluminum wall coverings, rugs, lampshades, store counters, wallpaper, record covers, cuff links, book jackets, mirror frames, shoe horns, coffee tables, shower stalls, and bottle openers. It now seems inevitable that a candy concoction labelled mosaic will be marketed.

This mass-production of facsimiles has obscured the fact that art performed the honors of introducing mosaic to America long before the Civil War. Perhaps one day the sociologists will explain it all; especially why any art only begins to have value to Americans if it reaches the sublime by first progressing through the ridiculous.

A MOSAIC IS A MOSAIC IS A MOSAIC: In early civilizations, the arts and crafts were an inseparable unit. In our time, however, we tend to think of mosaic in the categorical manner of a popular guessing game like "20 Questions"; i.e. anything made from vegetable (294, Corn Palace, Mitchell, S. D.), mineral (293, St. Mark's Cathedral, Venice, Italy), or animal (297, card stunts at a University of Southern California football game) employs the technique and therefore is a mosaic.* Obviously, this kind of labeling can become endless.

Most of these conflicting meanings began during the Renaissance when the separation of Church and State divided the arts from their crafts. The Industrial Revolution widened the gap, inventing special names to identify newly mechanized crafts. But no new word was coined for the *craft* of mosaic and so, in our time, mosaic has come to mean the *craft* more often than the *art*. Even more frequently, the term mosaic is misused in such a way as to imply an adaptation of the craft *is* the art. As heir to this divided concept, modern man is now rediscovering that mosaics have their greatest use and meaning (value and beauty) when the art and craft (form and function) are one.

Today, mosaics as a craft have found wide application as veneers for floors, ceilings, walls; as an art in integral-mosaics used to support structures; and as sculptural and transparent mediums. In all these methods, the final appearance of mosaic, either as works of art integrated within structures or as independent transportable panels, depends upon the needs of our architectural order. Since our industrial society is geometrically shaped in specific ways, the story of mosaic cannot be fully told without describing how our geometric or gridiron way of life in America formed our architectural order.

*The Encyclopedia Britannica states: The making of mosaics is the art of assembling units of materials (stone, marble, metal, smalti, wood, ivory, etc.) and inlaying them into another material such as marble, stone, concrete, wood, ivory, etc. When the area of such inlays is larger than the exposed surface of the supporting materials (which thus becomes the base or support to hold the pieces of inlay) the result can be called mosaic.

THE MOSAIC OF EVERYTHING AND EVERYBODY: How often have you heard the expression, "Don't be a Square!" used to needle someone for excessive stiffness or overformal behavior? Odd as it may seem, this everyday phrase reflects America's growing interest in the arts. Like all folklore, it is a humorous rejection of all those ideas in the 20th Century that still insist all play as well as work can be based on pure geometric order; that same kind of order necessary to run our machine-tooled world where everything is prefabricated out of a grid plan. Anyone who has taken a plane trip across America has observed the vast geometric mosaic of our life unfolding; a heritage of checkerboard farms and gridiron-planned cities, passing below one like some monumental graph stretching into infinity. From cradle to grave life we lived within this grid. It shapes how we develop the land, where we build, what we eat, when we sleep, and why we work.

Although sometimes this basic support can look and feel as menacing as. an armored girdle, it is the foundation of our own making, to do with what we will. Recently, the overwhelming pressures of growth within the grid have forced alterations. To save our cities from strangling in their own traffic, new freeways (299) are being built to go over, under, and right through the grid-planned city:

LONG BEFORE COLUMBUS DISCOVERED AMERICA: In Europe the radial city still prevails. Although tourists sometimes tend to regard the radial city as some sort of museum piece, it does let man live closer to nature. The art of mosaic grew up in this older agrarian or organic environment, starting with jewelry for royalty, and gradually progressing to a very developed art form. The Sumerians, Egyptians, Greeks, Romans, Early Christians, and citizens of Byzantium were familiar with mosaics done in everything from shells, metal, glass (296), and wood, to marble (301), stone, sand, and ivory. Nearly every conceivable scale, size, color, and shape of materials were tried at one time or another. The earliest mosaics were casual, decorative inventions based on organic shapes of nature. Slowly the art took on controlled, logical, and geometric forms as the first industrial methods grew out of the agrarian order of life familiar to the ancient world. The art of mosaic reached its Byzantine climax in the Cathedral of Hagia Sophia in Constantinople, a nearly perfect intermingling of East and West, with Christian philosophy acting as the catalyst.

THE TOTAL IMAGE OF BYZANTIUM: To those who have seen the splendor of Byzantine mosaics throughout Italy, it is not difficult to understand why this great era has captivated the contemporary mind. The organic unity of San Vitale in Ravenna, for example, is the superb work of an anonymous master-mosaicist who worked in a way almost unknown to the extremely individual artists of our time.

297

298

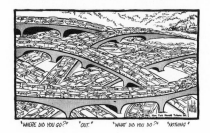

299

300

Having but a single philosophy to express, the master-mosaicist's problems of content and form were preordained. Also, since it was customary that he be well paid for his efforts, his mind was free to tackle the problems of creation. This was his main job and he did it by telling the story of the Bible on the walls of the church. He began by translating his scale color study to the walls by painting (in a pointillist manner that was to be rediscovered by Seurat, Pissarro and other French impressionists) with colors composed of raw pigment ground in lime-water. This rough fresco-type painting was done directly on the dried surface of the prepared setting bed (or scratch-coat of mortar).

The master-mosaicist's assistants, thoroughly trained to work as a team, then followed his bold color notation system (versus the outline system so often employed today) by first applying over the rough painting an additional coat of finer mortar made white with marble dust. This was done in patches from the top of the wall downward, and only as much as could be covered with tesserae within a half-hour, as the mortar set firm in that time. With a duplicate portion of the master's scale color-sketch in hand, and the master himself close by on the scaffolding to supervise, the assistant mosaicists selected colors with some degree of interpretation, and then pressed the stones directly into the cement.

Undoubtedly the master-mosaicist's supervision included holding the entire team of assistants within the over-all style, adjusting the light-reflecting angles of the stones to take advantage of the illumination, juxtaposing a contrasting color here and there to carry out the color vibration, and assuring consistency and quality of execution from day to day. Such an artist was truly a master of architectural scale. He, above all mosaicists who preceded and many who have followed, knew that the art of mosaic was more than an art of decoration.

EVERYBODY TALKS ABOUT THE WEATHER: Despite Mark Twain's famous remark, Byzantine mosaicists created materials able to do something about climatic conditions. In the Mediterranean countries, where heat and glaring sunlight are a problem, the builders of churches had to devise a means of keeping their large structures cool without shutting out all the light. It was solved by using smaller and often circular windows. This "funneling-in" of light through *bull's-eyes* was ideal for the use of glass mosaic; one of the few permanent materials flexible enough to express the purpose of the building while distributing the light.

Of course, the weather was just as important in the northern countries of Europe where the weak sunlight during the long winter made warmth and light desirable for the interiors of the large and drafty medieval cathedrals. Tapestries

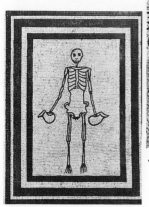

301

302

303

304

might be fine to lighten the gloom of a Hamlet living behind castle walls many feet thick, but the church as a sanctuary had less to fear, and could afford more light for the populace. It was the medieval artist who adapted the art of making mosaics to meet the problem of inadequate central heating. Instead of employing glass mosaics as a veneer with multiple functions, the opacity of mosaics was converted into the transparency of stained glass. Although temperatures inside the buildings only went up a few degrees, the Cathedrals looked warmer and attendance probably increased both in the North and in the South.

Despite all these practical accomplishments, the total image of the Byzantine and Medieval worlds crumbled with the rise of the Renaissance. Man turned back to ancient Rome and Greece for inspiration. Mosaics, so long in the service of the church, found itself without a patron. As all the arts became compartmentalized, mosaic was reduced to the survival level of a craft. Other than a few forlorn revivals, for hundreds of years the Goliath of art lay dormant.

HOW GILDED WAS OUR LILY? The use of mosaics in America, both as an art and craft, was very much influenced by immigration to the new world and the swift development of the tile industry. On the segregated level of fine arts, American architects before 1900 farmed out mosaic commissions to the workshops in Italy. It was an ornately imitative period and the artisans of Venice flourished, scaling the drawings and pasting the mosaic on paper to be shipped back to the United States for installation in prefabricated sections. The end result often revealed that architect and artisan were more than oceans apart, that is unless the architect undertook the role of an artist also and went to Venice to supervise the commission. Even then the crated mosaics sometimes got wet during the return voyage and arrived an indecipherable batch of mosaic swimming in dough-paste.

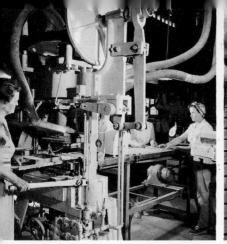

305

306

TOM SWIFT AND HIS MECHANICAL MOSAIC-MAKER! After 1900 the emigre tile and mosaic workers tried to adjust to the new industrial world of America by adapting their hand procedures to the swifter techniques of building. Setting mosaic by hand was quickly abandoned in favor of the man who operated a simple metal grid (304) and could set many square feet per day. Soon after, the man was replaced by the machine (305), and the change from the organic way of working to the geometric was complete. Since the art of mosaic was never suited to the manufacture of facsimiles from prototypes, the grid system substitute that was offered to replace mosaic had to be a mechanical checkerboard image.

As a result, before World War I, the term mosaic began to be used to describe tile work. Most of the workers in mosaic found they could make a better living installing terrazzo or tile imitations of mosaic; Greek floors for banks, Byzantine motifs for Turkish baths, and Roman fretwork for railway terminals. From concert hall foyers to hotel bathrooms the antiseptic white of thousands of tile installations moved through the growing cities of America like a giant glacier. Machine-made imitations of mosaic became so inexpensive they wound up gracing tenement house entrances.

The Industrial Revolution taught us to cover millions of square feet of flooring cheaply; however, the price included almost a quarter of a century without the rich color, texture, and art within authentic mosaic that helps make life more enjoyable. On the other side of the ledger must be recorded two important facts, both of which have indirectly benefited the art of mosaic. Just as the painter recognized the futility of competing with the camera, the mechanization of the tile industry has obviated competition between the mosaicists and the machine. Also, we must not forget that in many respects our tile industry is unsurpassed in the world today and, because of this accomplishment, has provided a fine new source of durable and inexpensive materials for the mosaicist.

The second period of mosaics in America coincided with the raccoon-coated prosperity of the 1920's. Architects and artists of that generation completed their education in Europe. When this avant-garde returned, the berets were put away, and among the architectural souvenirs brought back was a classical respect for mosaics.

Mosaics, instead of being restricted to flooring, were elevated to something one looked at. Framed wall areas in buildings were reserved for murals, and muralists were commissioned to design mosaics. As disciples of Blashfield, Brangwyn, or Parrish, they worked in the prevailing mode of their day. This meant being a facile manipulator of oil paints; anything more was not considered necessary since the 19th century academies of art had established the dictum that the execution of mosaics, true-fresco, and stained glass were crafts, and as such they were mediums a true maestro designed for, rather than worked with.

However, the sending off of mosaic designs for execution in Italy sometimes became too costly in terms of time, and so mosaic studios were started in America. Since most of the successful architects in the 1930's-1940's were very involved in the impossible task of recreating a dead past, the American mosaic workshops were seldom sought out to produce original works. The quality of artisanship in some shops excelled because they were supervised by artists who had taken the time to study in Europe and master the principles of creatively executing from their own designs. Too often the general quality of work seldom went beyond making skillful mosaics out of what should have remained uninspired paintings. The hopeful side to the American scene came with the end of World War II.

ART AS A BY-PRODUCT OF THE MACHINE! While the art of mosaic was living in a state of suspended animation in America on the fine arts level, it was being prepared for a metamorphosis on another and more important level; a rebirth via the unforeseen by-products of our mass-production system. The "division-of-labor" concept that nearly destroyed mosaic as an art, became the progenitor of a widespread and basic revival. As we have seen, until World War II the technical knowledge required to make mosaics had been relegated to a craft limited to a handful of mosaic workshops and tile contractors.

The revival of mosaics in Mexico, and 25 years of accumulated technological advances in America changed the scene overnight; less expensive pressed-glass mosaics were put on the world market as Italy's answer to America's keenly competitive tile industry; improvements in adhesives seemed to pour out of the laboratories, better cutting tools and supports were developed; more knowledge became available on mounting papers, colored grouts, and water-soluble glues.

After lying dormant for almost 400 years, the art of mosaic has begun to awaken throughout the world, returning as one of the most important integrating arts of the 20th century. In Mexico, Italy, France, Switzerland, Germany, and in America the accomplishments have taken on dimension and scope. Perhaps the 20th century has come full circle in history to pick up the values that were discarded by the Renaissance. Perhaps mankind has recognized the need of the symphonic light and color in mosaic to build a new total image. Perhaps the art once made by slaves for kings, and once used by the Church for the people, now will become one of the true arts of the people?

If this hopeful vista lies ahead, it is because of the increased leisure time which shorter working hours produced. During the depression few people imagined so many people would ever have the free time to discover there is more to recreation than sports, travel, and TV. Also, how few ever dreamed we would find ourselves a nation of skilled specialists forced to find our way back to hand arts we abandoned because we cannot afford to hire our counterparts? These are some of the forces that brought forth the "do-it-yourself" movement in America and what better example than mosaic kits?

HOW FAR CAN PROGRESS PROGRESS? Almost anybody can do a creditable mosaic, if a reasonable amount of time is devoted to learning the craft. The colors are so bright and clean, one can also be easily misled into doing badly conceived and executed mosaics. Mosaic kits have both of these possibilities, i.e., while none can honestly claim they will teach you to do a masterpiece, many do offer the convenience of assembled materials and tools. Anything that encourages people to become genuinely involved in the creative experiences of art is a healthy thing; one must make certain it is actually art and not a facsimile being passed off as art. When it comes to mosaic kits, the danger of a facsimile begins when the manufacturer is not content to offer tools and materials, but throws in instructions and sets of designs to copy. It would be wonderful if these were *creative* in approach, but, more often than not, they are mediocre, trite designs pretending to teach through technique alone.

No one can measure the harm done by encouraging people to believe they can create art by buying a kit that distorts the fundamentals of the craft; i.e., because this approach generally starts the beginner with copying someone else's designs. It has nothing to offer the beginner interested in developing his own creativity. It is most important to examine the merits of a kit by first looking at the quality of tools and materials provided. Then check which authority in the field of professional mosaicists did the manufacturer employ to design and assemble the kit. More concretely, Gino Severini, the great Italian mosaicist (see page 101), summed up this point when he said, "Ancient mosaics have aroused much interest and admiration because of the perfect union of art and craft. In the work of today, unfortunately, this accord is often missing. It cannot possibly exist if the art is done by one person and craft by another." If the future of automation in the United States will give enough people more time to trust the artist in themselves, then progress will progress pretty far.

STATUS QUO VADIS: Alongside this growing enthusiasm to participate in the arts are many architectural artists throughout the world who deserve the attention of every student of mosaic. Antonio Gaudi, the great Spanish architect, whose integration of mosaic and form in La Sagra Familia Cathedral in Barcelona is admired by sculptors and mosaicists as well as architects. Thousands of visitors to Rome have discovered Pietro and Annamaria Cascella's magnificent mosaic mural in the railway terminal. Unfortunately, it is also true that most of the professional world of art and architecture is manacled by a *status quo vadis* concept and lives by the premise that all art is not one. The creative uses of mosaic have always been dependent upon the existence of an imaginative architectural order, an order that fulfills all human needs by employing the directional character of great artists.

In Southern California's famed Los Angeles, there are many miles between the oil rigs covering the Baldwin Hills, Lloyd Wright's Wayfarer Chapel on Portuguese Bend, and Simon Radilla's strange mosaic towers in Watts (309). And yet all these seemingly unrelated works are very important to the future of mosaic; especially if viewed as the legitimate grandchildren of Paxton's Cyrstal Palace in London of a century ago, or the Galleria in Milan, the Eiffel Tower in Paris, and the Brooklyn Bridge in New York. Throughout these remarkable structures the advantages of lighter and stronger supporting members were used. The structural wall was eliminated, or glass substituted, and imaginative engineering opened up possibilities for the future.

However, this left only the beams, glass, floors and ceilings as workable surfaces for the artist, unless the building was completely enclosed to be serviced by electricity and airconditioning. While engineers like Buckminster Fuller of the United States, Pier Luigi Nervi of Italy, and Felix Candela of Mexico have been furthering a more organic approach to architecture, the artistic potential of the "open" structure was first sensed by a self-educated artist named Simon Radilla. For 25 years Simon Radilla covered the supporting members of his fantastic, 100 foot towers with mosaic made from the discarded crockery and bottles found on junk-heaps.

Recently Nicholas Schoeffer, without having seen the Radilla Towers, used sound in addition to color and form in his "spatio-dynamic" tower for a park in Paris. In the field of transparent screen-walls for buildings, many artists have been at work.* And where the enclosed structure is paramount, the opaque modular-mosaics in stone by Mexico's Juan O'Gorman demonstrate the ability of an artist to dominate

*Jan de Swart, Emile Norman, Robert Mallory, Sam Kaner, Ray Rice, Roger Darricarrere, etc.

307

308

310

309

311

the grid system and make it support a functional expression. Now that some of the extremes of opacity and transparency have been explored, most likely a synthesis of these elements will formulate the new direction in the art of making mosaics.

The general public, and particularly the professional world of art, must look to the creative architectural artists of our time if the gridiron system is to be used as a means to expression. Today, the gridiron system often appears to be the end aspiration in the arts. However, as the means and ends are harmonized, all these specialized and segregated concepts within the world of art will be absorbed into a total image of our society. If our time is to face this challenge, our artists will have to expand the meaning and purpose of art until it can provide science with the kind of goals that will integrate the diverse directions of man.

BIBLIOGRAPHY

BOOKS

Anthony, E. W. *A History of Mosaics*. Boston: Porter Sargent, 1935.

Avi-Yonah, M. and Shapiro, M. *Israel, Ancient Mosaics*. Greenwich: New York Graphic Society, 1960.

Bitterman, Eleanor. *Art in Modern Architecture*. New York: Reinhold, 1952.

Bovini, Giuseppe. *Ravenna Mosaics*. Greenwich: New York Graphic Society, 1956.

Carls, E. W. and Wines, L. S. *The Art of Tile Setting*. Peoria: Charles Bennett Co., 1954.

Cennini, Cennino. *The Craftsman's Handbook*. Translated by D. V. Thompson. New York: Dover, 1959.

Course in Tilesetting: Parts I and II. Sacramento: California State Department of Education, 1958.

Damaz, Paul. *Art in European Architecture*. New York: Reinhold, 1956.

Damaz, Paul. *Art in Latin American Architecture*. New York: Reinhold, 1963.

Diamond, Freda. *The Story of Glass*. New York: Harcourt, Brace and World, 1953.

Graber, Andre. *Byzantine Painting*. New York: Skira, 1953.

Graf, Don. *Thin Setting Bed Methods and Materials*. New York: Tile Council of America, 1952.

Graf, Don. *Tile Handbook*. New York: Tile Council of America, 1951.

Greece: Byzantine Mosaics. ("UNESCO World Art Series," Vol. 13.) New York: UNESCO Publications, 1959.

Herberts, Kurt. *The Complete Book of Artists' Techniques*. New York: Frederick A. Praeger, 1958.

Jackson, F. Hamilton. *Intarsia and Marquetry*. London: Sand and Co., 1903.

Journal of Glass Studies: Vols. I, II, III and IV. Corning, New York: Corning Museum of Glass, 1962.

Maclehose, L. B. *Vasari on Technique*. New York: Dover, 1961.

Maiuri, Amadeo. *Roman Painting*. New York: Skira, 1953.

Neuberg, Frederic. *Glass in Antiquity*. London: Art Trade Press, 1949.

Solon, Leon V. *Polychromy*. New York: Architectural Record, 1924.

Stieri, Emanuele. *Concrete and Masonry*. New York: Barnes and Noble, 1956.

Sweeney, J. J. and Sert, J. L. *Antonio Gaudi*. New York: Frederick A. Praeger, 1960.

Toesco and Forlate. *Mosaics of St. Marks*. Greenwich: New York Graphic Society, 1958.

Turquoise Mosaic Art in Ancient Mexico. New York: Museum of the American Indian, Heye Foundation, 1922.

PERIODICALS

Baker, Harriet E. "Mosaics of Sumer," *Creative Crafts* (June/July, 1960).

Beaman, R. B. "Fused Glass Murals," *Stained Glass* (Spring, 1961).

Binning, B. C. "Mosaics: Vancouver to Venice," *Canadian Art* (November, 1958).

Bradbury, R. "Mosaic Art in Modern Architecture," *Craft Horizons* (September, 1957).

Brooks, P. K. "Tiles and Mosaics in Advertising," *American Artist* (June, 1955).

Bruton, H. "How to Make Pebble Mosaics," *House Beautiful* (July, 1954).

Buchanan, D. W. "New Murals and Mosaics in Mexico," *Canadian Art* (1951).

"A Buried Treasure Is Brought to Light," *Fortune* (December, 1960).

Campbell, L. "Jeanne Reynal: Mosaic as Architecture," *Craft Horizons* (January, 1962).

Centili, G. V. "Roman Life in 1600 Year Old Color Pictures," *National Geographic* (February, 1957).

Clark, A. W. "Making Modern Ceramic Mosaics," *School Arts* (May, 1956).

Clow, Bard. "Venetian Glass," *Craft Horizons* (July/August, 1956).

Crimi, A. "Making a Mosaic Mural," *American Artist* (February, 1962).

Dockstader, Frederick. "The Pre-Columbian Art of Mosaic," *Creative Crafts* (June/July, 1960).

Edward, J. "Dick Seeger: Artist-Craftsman in Plastics," *Creative Crafts* (July/August, 1962).

Frankl, Gerard J. R. "How Cézanne Saw and Used Color," *BBC Listener* (October 25, 1961).

Frere, S. "Lifting Mosaics," *Antiquity* (June, 1958).

Friedman, B. H. "Manhattan Mosaic," *Craft Horizons* (January/February, 1959).

Howard, T. "Tiles, Faience and Mosaic in Modern Building," *Royal Institute of British Architects* (September, 1955).

Karlikow, Abe. "Gemmaux: Painting in Glass," *Craft Horizons* (December, 1957).

Lovoos, Janice. "Mary Bowling: Intarsiast," *Creative Crafts* (November/December, 1961).

Lyon, M. "Art and Craft of Making Mosaics," *House Beautiful* (August, 1955).

"Memorial in Mosaic to U.S. War Dead," *Life* (August 24, 1958).

Millet, F. and Cox, O. "Mural Techniques Today," *Architectural Review* (August, 1961).

"Mosaics by Juan O'Gorman," *Arts and Architecture* (February, 1959).

"Mosaics from Bits of Colored Tile," *Ceramics Monthly* (January, 1955).

"Mosaics in Translucent Plastic," *Sunset* (March, 1956).

Norman, James. "Juan O'Gorman's Mosaic Mural," *American Artist* (June, 1953).

"Proud Byzantium's Treasure," *Life* (December, 1950).

"Revival in Mosaics," *House and Garden* (December, 1956).

Rudd, M. "How to Make Pebbled Mosaics for Garden Paths and Patios," *House and Garden* (May, 1953).

"Sahl Swarz Makes a New Approach to an Ancient Art," *American Artist* (June, 1955).

Smith, Dido. "Gold Glass: An Ancient Technique Rediscovered," *Craft Horizons* (December, 1956).

"Stained Glass Now a Craft," *Sunset Western Living* (March, 1963).

Steinitz, Kate. "Fantastic Architecture," *Artforum* (August, 1962).

Uchida, Y. "Eggshell Mosaics," *Craft Horizons* (March, 1962).

Von Eckhardt, Wolf. "Transiucent Beauty," *AIA Journal* (February, 1962).

Webster, J. C. "The Technique of Impressionism," *College Art Journal* (November, 1944).

ARTICLES ON THE WORK OF JOSEPH L. YOUNG

Adlow, Dorothy. "Bas-relief Mosaic Mural by Joseph Young," *Christian Science Monitor* (April 11, 1962).

"Joseph L. Young," *Current Biography* (July, 1960).

"California Muralist Wins National Recognition," *Architecture and Engineering* (March, 1954).

"Church Dignitaries Dedicate Mural," *Tile Magazine* (October, 1956).

"Exhibition by Joseph L. Young at Falk-Raboff Gallery," *Art News* (April, 1953).

Howell, Betje. "A New Mural by Joseph Young," *Creative Crafts* (March/April, 1962).

Lovoos, Janice. "Mosaic Murals," *American Artist* (February, 1962).

"Major Mosaic Mural Project for Temple," *Tile Magazine* (April, 1956).

"Mosaic Arch for Memorial Park," *Tile and Architectural Ceramics* (January, 1961).

"Mosaics Honor 12 Tribes of Israel at Memorial," *Midwest Magazine, Chicago Sun* (April 15, 1962).

"Mosaics of Joseph Young," *Architectural Record* (June, 1957).

Sewell, E. K. "Joseph Young Creates a Unique Mosaic Mural," *American Artist* (September, 1955).

ARTICLES BY JOSEPH L. YOUNG

"Arts and Crafts in Architecture," *Creative Crafts* (May/June, 1961).

"Doing a Wall Panel in the Direct Method," *Popular Ceramics* (May, 1960).

"Glassmaking in Murano," *Creative Crafts* (September/October, 1962).

"Mosaics: an Ancient Art Revives," *Popular Ceramics* (January, 1960).

"Mosaics, Merchandising and Mediocrity," *Creative Crafts* (June/July, 1960).

"Murano Revisited," *Creative Crafts* (May/June, 1961).

"Practical Mosaic Craft," *Design* (March, 1948).

"The Art of Mosaics," *Popular Ceramics* (February, 1960)

"The Walls of America," *Charette* (October, 1950).

"Why Mosaics Are Not Painting in Glass," Parts I and II, *Popular Ceramics* (March and April, 1960).

FILMS

"Ceramic Tile in Modern School Design," by Tile Council of America, New York (35mm, color and sound, 35 minutes).

"Film Exercise No. 1 (Watts Towers)," by Bayliss Glascock, Los Angeles, California (16mm, color and sound, 6 minutes, 1962).

"Glass," by Bert Haanstra (16mm, color and sound, 12 minutes, 1958).

"How to Get Better Tile Installations," by Tile Council of America, New York (35mm, color and sound, 20 minutes).

"Inventive Design," by Tile Council of America, New York (35mm, color and sound).

"Mosaic Experiments," by Robert Longini, Immaculate Heart College, Los Angeles, California (16mm, color and sound, 20 minutes, 1957).

"The World of Mosaic," by the University of California at Los Angeles (16mm, color and sound, 28 minutes, 1957. Narrated by Richard Widmark, featuring the mosaics of Joseph L. Young).

"The Towers," by William Hale, Los Angeles, California (16mm, color and sound, 12 minutes, 1953).

35mm COLOR SLIDES AND FILM STRIPS

"Mosaics by Joseph Young and Others," including University of Mexico City, by J. Barry O'Rourke, Los Angeles, California, 1962.

"Mosaics for All," by Immaculate Heart College, Los Angeles, California (three 16mm color filmstrips, 1957).

PHOTO CREDITS

INDEX